By The Editors of Consumer Guide®

Library of Congress Catalog Card Number: 79-67763

This edition published by:
Beekman House
A Division Of Crown Publishers, Inc.
One Park Avenue
New York, N.Y. 10016

Chief Contributing Author: Richard M. Langworth
Contributing Authors: Rick Kopec, Michael Lamm, Paul G. McLaughlin

Cover Design: Frank E. Peiler
Photo Credits: Ford Motor Company Photomedia Department and Design Center; Richard M. Langworth; Sports Car Club of America

A Fitting Introduction

For me, the excitement in the automobile business is to do something different; to pioneer a new concept, and to win.

Years ago, some of us believed that America was ready for a new kind of car. It would be a small, personal type of car that the average American could afford and would enjoy. It had to be classic in style, yet should immediately imply performance. We reached way out, and the success that Mustang has enjoyed is proof that Americans really like something which is entirely new and dramatically different.

Lee A. Iacocca

Lee A. Iacocca
Chairman, Chrysler Corporation

Contents

Developing the Personal Car:1946~64

The evolution of the Ford Mustang did not begin in 1962 with the experimental Mustang I, or in 1955 with the first two-seat Thunderbird, though both of these cars have a place in the Mustang story. The Mustang tale really begins with developments in the auto industry as early as 1946 when America was emerging from World War II into an age of unbridled optimism.

When car production resumed shortly after the war, it was impossible for the auto manufacturers to offer an all-new model. The prewar body dies were still practically unused so it was uneconomical to scrap them. Besides, there wasn't time to design and re-tool completely fresh designs. So the industry opened the 1946 model year with cars that were simply warmed-over 1942 designs. Of course, at that time a company could sell literally anything on wheels, so there was little incentive to introduce a truly new model right away. Only Studebaker, among the prewar makes, was entirely redesigned for 1947. But as time went on, the seller's market waned as a war-starved public's appetite for new cars was satiated. Soon, buyers began hungering for new engineering and styling developments. Indeed, the manufacturers themselves had baited the public throughout the war with promises of brand-new designs that would appear as soon as hostilities ended. However, it wasn't until 1949 that the Big Three—Ford, Chrysler, and General Motors—offered entirely new designs from each of their divisions.

In rushing their prewar cars into production immediately after the war, some manufacturers began to consider how these designs, which by now were familiar to the public, could be made to appear new, at least on the surface. One idea was to create a few "limited-production" specials based on the holdover prewar models to maintain public interest until the company's all-new cars could be brought to market.

In 1946 Chrysler, Ford, and Nash each produced such limited-production specials. Based on conventional production bodies, all of these cars were embellished with wooden exterior trim which used a framework made of white ash, maple, or yellow birch with mahogany wood or mahogany decal inserts.

Two of these specials, the Nash Suburban and the Chrysler Town & Country, were sedans built on wheelbases about 10 feet long. Each was powered by a middle-sized L-head six. Chrysler also offered a Town & Country convertible built on an even longer wheelbase and equipped with an eight-cylinder engine. Chrysler sold over 12,000 Town & Countrys during 1946-48, while Nash sold 1,000 of its Suburbans. These models served their purpose of maintaining floor traffic in dealer showrooms until the all-new Chryslers and Nashes were introduced for 1949. Although Nash dropped the Suburban model that year, Chrysler continued the Town & Country convertible in 1949 and added a hardtop version for the 1950 model year. After 1950, the Town & Country simply became a name used for Chrysler station wagons.

The first limited editions created by the makers of the future Mustang were the Ford and Mercury Sportsman convertibles of 1946. These cars were inspired by a customized Model A built by then-styling director Bob Gregorie. Henry Ford II, just released from the Navy and ready to help salvage his ailing company, was searching for something different to offer the public. After seeing Gregorie's wood-trimmed Model A, Henry II ordered a similar treatment for the production 1946 convertible, and the Sportsman went into production. Finding the planking was no problem for Ford since the company owned a stand of timber in Northern Michigan which was used to supply wood for the wagon bodies.

The Mercury Sportsman appeared only in 1946, when a mere 205 cars were sold. The Sportsman was built on a longer wheelbase and was heavier than Ford's version. Since the Mercury shared the Ford's 100-hp flathead V-8 engine, it did not perform as well as its stablemate. Mercury dropped its Sportsman in 1947. The car was priced over $200 more than its Ford counterpart, and the Sportsman did not significantly contribute to Mercury sales traffic.

The Ford Sportsman, however, was a minor sales success. Close to 3,500 were sold each year between 1946 and 1948. Although such figures were not significant from a sales standpoint, the car generated extra publicity for the rest of Ford's carryover postwar line. The Sportsman was phased out early in 1948, since Ford was preparing all-new designs for 1949 and no longer needed a special model to add zest to its image.

By 1950, however, Ford was back in the business of producing limited editions. That year's specials were called the Ford Custom Deluxe Crestliner and the Mercury Monterey. Each was essentially a customized version of the standard two-door sedan. The Crestliner featured a two-tone color scheme (a contrasting color

1946 Chrysler Town & Country

1946 Ford Sportsman

1946 Nash Suburban

1950 Ford Custom Deluxe Crestliner

1950 Mercury Monterey

1949 Kaiser Virginian

sweep was used along the lower body) and a padded vinyl top. The Monterey offered a choice of padded tops in canvas or leather plus a deluxe interior. The idea behind both cars was to simulate the appearance of a true convertible with its feeling of sportiness. The Crestliner and Monterey were designed as a substitute for the pillarless "hardtop convertible" body style introduced by GM in 1949, which was already selling at a rapid clip.

Responding more directly to the sales threat from the GM hardtops, Ford then introduced the Victoria pillarless coupe in 1951, and dropped the Crestliner. Mercury and Lincoln, however, still lacked a hardtop, so Mercury continued with the Monterey, and Lincoln added similar customs, called the Lido and Capri, to its line. None of these limited editions were particularly successful, however, and when the redesigned 1952 Lincoln and Mercury were announced, true hardtops appeared and the padded-top specials were deleted.

The Monterey and Capri designations continued as series names in the Mercury and Lincoln lines, respectively.

Aside from the Nash Suburban, there were no noteworthy postwar limited editions from the independent car makers until 1949. In that year upstart Kaiser-Frazer, the new auto company which began production after the war in Willow Run, Michigan, entered the field with its Kaiser Virginian, followed a few years later by K-F's unusual Kaiser Dragons.

The Virginian was merely the result of a prior management decision to make a convertible out of K-F's conventional four-door sedan. But its engineering was of the patchwork variety, demonstrated by K-F's use of a ponderous reinforced frame to prevent body flex. The Virginian was really the first "four-door convertible sedan," although it had small, metal-framed glass pillars that did not roll down out of sight. A fixed-roof Virginian was also offered. Like the Ford

Crestliner, this so-called "hardtop" offered an optional roof styled to resemble a convertible top and most cars were fitted with this. But at a price of $3,000, the Kaiser Virginian was prohibitively expensive for its day and only about 1,000 were sold through 1950.

The "personal Kaiser" for 1951 was the Dragon, which was offered initially as a trim variation for the top-line Kaiser Deluxe. The first Dragons were distinguished from other Kaiser models only by their interiors. Seats, door panels, and dashboard padding were trimmed in embossed "dragon vinyl," (the name "dragon" was used to avoid confusion with the skin of alligators whose survival was, even then, of concern to ecologists). The Dragon was the first car from a major manufacturer to use embossed vinyl as an upholstery material, thereby setting a trend that would quickly spread throughout the industry.

Later in 1951, K-F offered a "Mark II" Dragon with a vinyl top as well as a vinyl interior. The pattern was now called "dinosaur vinyl" (there would be no mistaking this one for the hide of any endangered species). A later version, with bamboo-like vinyl trim, was known appropriately as the Jade Dragon. Although these cars were slow sellers, they at least kept customers coming in.

Kaiser skipped a limited edition model for 1952, but in 1953 it revived the series as the "Hardtop Dragon." Taking a cue from Ford, K-F promoted this four-door sedan as a hardtop by virtue of its padded "bambu vinyl" top. Richly upholstered, the 1953 Dragons were embellished with gold-plated medallions, hood ornament, and a gold owner's nameplate for the dash. At about $3,800 each, they didn't sell well. Less than 1,300 were built, and many were left over at the end of the model year.

But 1953 was a good year for limited edition "personal cars" other than the Dragon. Packard, for example, offered a svelte new convertible called the Caribbean. This car took many of its styling themes from the interesting Pan American two-seater, which was developed for publicity purposes with the Henney Body Company in 1952 under the hard-driving leadership of Packard's new president James J. Nance. Priced at $5,200 and equipped with a potent 180-hp straight eight, the Caribbean was distinguished from the standard Packard convertibles by its ultra-clean lines and a custom hood having a full-width air scoop. Elegantly trimmed, it was the star attraction at Packard showrooms. The Caribbean continued in production for 1954, and used an even larger 212-hp engine. Caribbean output was small—750 in 1953, and only 400 in 1954—but the car was an important prestige offering. It convinced customers that Packard was serious about regaining its luxury image.

The Caribbean was restyled for 1955 and fitted with a new 275-hp V-8. In 1956, horsepower rose again to 310. Convertible prices remained at around $6,000; a companion Caribbean hardtop priced at $5,500 was added for 1956. But falling sales of Packard's other higher-volume models, and financial losses following Packard's purchase of Studebaker in 1954, con-

1953 Kaiser "Hardtop" Dragon

1953 Packard Caribbean

1953 Oldsmobile Fiesta

1953 Cadillac Eldorado

demned the Caribbean to extinction by 1957.

Certainly the strongest exponent of the "personal car" theme in the early '50s was General Motors. In 1953, GM introduced limited-production specials in four of its five divisions: the Cadillac Eldorado, Buick Skylark, Oldsmobile Fiesta, and Chevrolet Corvette. Their main purpose was to test public reaction to certain styling and engineering ideas that might be used on future mass production models.

The $5,700 Oldsmobile Fiesta had a custom leather interior, a 170-hp version of the Rocket V-8 engine, and was one of the first production cars to have a wraparound windshield. Standard equipment also included Hydra-Matic transmission and power-assisted brakes, steering, windows, and seats. Only 458 Fiestas were produced. The model was dropped for 1954 because management decided a limited edition did not appeal to the typical Olds buyer who was thought to be somewhat less interested in "personal expression" than a Buick or Cadillac buyer.

Buick's Skylark was a more ambitious project than the Fiesta. It was a sectioned, chopped, and channeled Buick convertible four inches shorter and more cleanly styled than the standard Buicks. It sported Kelsey-Hayes wire wheels and the finest quality upholstery. Buick built only 1,690 Skylarks in 1953 and sold them for $5,000 each. The Skylark returned in 1954, but its price was cut to $4,500, and many of its exclusive styling features disappeared. Only 836 copies of the '54 model were sold, and Buick dropped the Skylark from its lineup for 1955.

The Cadillac Eldorado was the most successful GM personal car of the '50s, and later it would strongly influence the product planners at Ford. Priced at what seemed like an astronomical $7,750, the '53 Eldorado was established as an upper-crust specialty car and only 532 were sold that first year. Like the Skylark, the '53 Eldorado used a cut-down convertible body and a wraparound windshield. A metal cover, which concealed the convertible top when stowed, gave a smooth look to the rear deck. For 1954, Cadillac decided to capitalize on the Eldorado's prestige by making the car more saleable. Its price was cut by $2,000, and it used a standard Cadillac convertible body. The new car lacked the unique custom styling of the 1953 version, but its lower price sparked sales. The division sold 2,000 Eldorados in 1954, 4,000 in 1955, and 6,000 in 1956. Eldorados were easily distinguished from other Cadillacs by distinctive rear-end styling that featured sharply pointed fins. From 1956 on, the Eldorado engine was always slightly more powerful than the standard V-8 used in other Cadillacs. For 1957-58, Cadillac fielded another specialty car, the $13,000 Eldorado Brougham close-coupled sedan. Eldorado sales picked up in the early '60s and rose to significant levels by 1967, when a new Eldorado was introduced. Equipped with the front-wheel-drive system of the Olds Toronado, this new generation Eldorado became one of the most successful high-priced personal cars in history. Not surprisingly, it is still with us today.

But the public's taste wasn't limited just to big, flashy convertibles and hardtops. By the mid-1950's, the sports car had also captured America's fancy. Returning GI's had brought home MGs and Jaguars from England. The popularity of these cars led the Europeans to design other sports cars aimed squarely at the tastes of American buyers—the Triumph TR2, Austin-Healey 100, Alfa Romeo Giulietta, Mercedes-Benz 190SL. Although sports car sales accounted for

1951 Nash-Healey

1954 Kaiser-Darrin

1954 Hudson Italia

1954 Chevrolet Corvette

only .027 percent of the American market in 1953, the public in general seemed fascinated by European features like bucket seats, floor-mounted manual gearshifts, and lithe two-seater bodies. Detroit's marketing mavens began to wonder whether a sports car in the lineup might help sales even more than customized editions of production models.

Two sports models from independent manufacturers had been launched by 1953—the Nash-Healey, which debuted in 1951, and the Kaiser-Darrin, which arrived in 1953 as a 1954 model. Another sporting entry was the very low-volume Hudson Italia of 1954-55, a four-seat grand tourer based on the compact Hudson Jet. But the independents simply weren't financially able to produce or sell these cars. They had to be more concerned with the success of higher-volume family cars on which their profits and survival depended.

Chevrolet's Corvette, on the other hand, was a product of the highest-selling single make and the most successful corporation in the world. Powered by a mediocre six-cylinder engine and automatic transmission, and having an unorthodox fiberglass body complete with old-fashioned side curtains, the 1953 Corvette was really more of a tourer than a sports car. MG and Triumph fans were appalled by the Corvette's trendy styling and automatic gearbox. Those who admired Eldorados didn't like its plastic side curtains and limited luggage and passenger space. At one point, around 1954-55, GM actually considered dropping the Corvette altogether. Fortunately for future Corvette fans, GM decided to develop the car further. The first V-8-engine Corvettes arrived in 1955, followed in 1956 by smooth new styling from the pen of Harley Earl, and then fuel injection in 1957. The Corvette was soon transformed into a true sports car, and enjoyed increasing sales success into the '60s and '70s.

At Ford Motor Company's Dearborn headquarters, where every General Motors move was carefully watched, the Corvette was the subject of much debate. In 1953, Ford was in the midst of a historic comeback.

The disorganized company of 1945 had been built into a dynamic GM competitor by chairman Henry Ford II and president Ernest Breech. It was traditional for Ford to respond to any product innovation from General Motors with a model of its own. But should Ford field a challenger to the low-volume Corvette?

The arrival of the first production Corvettes helped Ford reach a decision. According to former Ford product planner Tom Case, "There wasn't any question about it. Mr. Ford wanted a civilized sports car, if we were going to build a two-seater at all. The Corvette was too spartan, too much like an MG. You just couldn't imagine Mr. Ford struggling to raise one of those plastic side curtains." The company's response appeared in due course at the end of 1954—the Thunderbird.

The 1955 Thunderbird was pushed into production by Henry Ford's lieutenant, Lewis B. Crusoe, general manager of Ford Division. Crusoe was a marketing man first and a car buff second. As a result, the first Thunderbird was primarily a brilliant marketing maneuver designed to outflank the Corvette. In its early design phases Crusoe decreed the new car would have a V-8 engine: A six-cylinder powerplant would not even be offered. The V-8 chosen turned out to be a 292 cubic-inch unit with close to 200 hp. Crusoe also wanted the Thunderbird to offer an optional automatic transmission and an optional hardtop. A deluxe interior package complete with conventional roll-up windows was also planned from the start. Thunderbird styling, which was largely the work of Ford designers Robert Maguire and Damon Woods, was spectacular. Priced

1955 Ford Thunderbird

1957 Ford Thunderbird

1956 Ford Thunderbird

1957 Continental Mark II

at $2,944, the 1955 T-Bird was competitive with the 1955 Corvette V-8. Given buyer preferences for luxury features, the outcome was predictable: In 1955 Chevrolet sold 675 Corvettes; Ford sold 16,155 Thunderbirds.

Styling for the 1956 Thunderbird was a mild face-lift of the 1955 design. The 1957 edition, however, was more extensively reworked. The '57 T-Bird gained a combination bumper-grille, modest tailfins, and a revised interior. Horsepower was increased up to 300 hp for the 1957 models. Sales for 1956 were 15,631; for 1957 they rose to 21,380. But even as the 1955 Thunderbird was introduced, an all-new four-seat model was being prepared for the 1958 model year.

The marketing decisions which influenced the evolution of the Thunderbird's design are crucial to the Mustang story, for as Tom Case likes to say, "the Mustang was really the original Thunderbird revived—with two extra seats."

The story of how the two-seat T-Bird became the four-seat Mustang began after Crusoe moved up in the company hierarchy. His place as general manager was taken by Robert F. McNamara, who later became U.S. Secretary of Defense, and is now president of the World Bank. A no-nonsense financial man, McNamara decided that Ford Motor Company would no longer build cars regardless of their sales potential. Instead, everything Ford built from then on was going to be designed primarily to make money. If the car was also interesting, so much the better.

The effects of McNamara's policies reached far beyond Ford Division alone and soon he was exerting a real influence on top corporate management. At Lincoln-Mercury, for example, a Mercury production man was brought in to make recommendations on how the exclusive Continental Mark II could be built and sold more profitably. Priced at $10,000, the Mark II had been Ford's ultimate car in 1956-57—but the company lost about $1,000 on every one it sold. Under McNamara's direction the 1958 Continental Mark III was designed to share components with the standard higher-volume 1958 Lincoln cars. As a result, the '58 Mark III became far less distinctive, but it was also much cheaper to build than was the Mark II, and for the first time, the Continental made a profit.

At Ford Division, making money was even more important, aside from its perennial rivalry with Chevrolet. The flashy but slow-selling 1955-56 Ford Crown Victoria which featured an optional—and costly—transparent plastic roof, was eliminated from the line in 1957. The novel Ford Skyliner, a convertible which featured a retractable steel roof instead of a folding cloth top, was already in the design stage when McNamara arrived at Ford and he was too late to stop it from going into production. But when the Skyliner failed to sell in significant numbers for three successive seasons, he axed it for 1960.

As for the future of the Thunderbird, McNamara had three basic options. He could continue the car in its two-seat form as a prestige item, and sell it at a loss or perhaps at a small profit. He could also drop it entirely.

Or he could remake the T-Bird into something that would sell in greater quantities than the two-seater. Given McNamara's orientation to designing cars that would make a profit, the choice was obvious: A four-seat Thunderbird would debut for the 1958 model year. He also adamantly refused to continue the existing two-seater as a companion model. A two-seater, he felt, would divert attention away from the new, larger car, which would need to have maximum impact to stimulate initial sales.

Even before the decision was made to drop it, the two-seat Thunderbird had been established as a car with a vastly different character from the Corvette's. Instead of being a race-and-ride sports car, which the Corvette definitely was after 1955, the T-Bird was a "boulevard sports car." Though it looked sporty, it handled with little more agility than a standard Ford Fairlane. Thunderbirds were rarely seen in competition, where they were not very successful anyway. But because it combined the allure of a sports car with the special styling and luxury features of the limited

1958 Ford Skyliner

1958 Ford Thunderbird

1958 Ford Thunderbird

1964 Studebaker Gran Turismo Hawk

1965 Corvair Corsa

1958 Cadillac Eldorado Brougham

1963 Buick Riviera

Prototype for 1962 Corvair convertible

1962 Chrysler 300

editions dating back to the Ford Sportsman, Thunderbird outsold Corvette handily. Even so, the two-seater's annual sales rate of 15,000 to 20,000 units was too low for McNamara. The four-seater T-Bird would have to triple or quadruple the two-seater's sales figures to earn a permanent place in the Ford line.

McNamara's decision was proven correct. The 1958 four-seat Thunderbird was a sweeping sales success. A new unit body was designed for the car, which was offered as a convertible or a fixed hardtop. To make up for its added weight compared to the two-seater, the 1958 Thunderbird had a more powerful 300-hp, 352 cubic-inch V-8 engine as standard equipment. T-Bird production for 1958 was around 40,000 units; the vast majority of these were hardtops. In 1960, Thunderbird production exceeded 90,000 units. After 1963, the

T-Bird became more of a luxury car than a grand tourer, but it never lost the cachet of "personal luxury" established by the '58 "Squarebird." That image had strong appeal for moneyed customers, who would never have been satisfied with a two-seater.

Unlike the limited editions or other personal cars before it, the four-seat Thunderbird design was fresh from the ground up and created specifically for its market. It was intended not only to build showroom traffic, but was also designed to sell in high volume. Its success was not lost on the competition. Chrysler was soon adding four bucket seats and a center console to its high performance "letter-series" 300s. General Motors quickly launched a squadron of "personal" or "performance" models from its various divisions, such as the luxurious, bucket-seated 1961 Oldsmobile

Starfire, to do battle with the T-Bird. Except for Cadillac's Eldorado Brougham, however, none of the GM specials was a completely new design. It wasn't until 1963 that GM produced the elegant Buick Riviera, conceived expressly by styling chief William L. Mitchell to compete with the Thunderbird.

Studebaker, too, copied the Thunderbird product package with its 1962-64 Gran Turismo Hawk. The Hawk GTs were beautiful cars which had been cleverly created out of Studebaker's nearly ten-year-old hardtop bodyshell by designer Brooks Stevens. With a roofline taken directly from the Thunderbird, Hawks could be equipped with features like those of European grand touring cars, such as a four-speed gearbox, disc brakes, and supercharged V-8 engine. But Studebaker was in dire financial trouble by the early 1960's, and the GT Hawk did not sell as well as it deserved.

The early sales success of the four-passenger Thunderbirds combined with continuing buyer interest in sports cars suggested a new market segment for Detroit in the early '60s—the sporty, low-priced, compact. The first of these was the 1960 Corvair Monza, introduced late in the model year as a trim option for Chevrolet's rear-engine economy car. Successful beyond even GM's projections, the Monza single-handedly kept the Corvair in production for the next ten years. The original 1960 model was too unconventional for the public and, as an economy car, did not sell well against Ford's ultra-simple Falcon. After two years of slow Corvair sales, Chevy launched its own conventional front-engine, live-axle Chevy II to compete with the Falcon in 1962. But the Monza, because of its vinyl bucket seats, full carpeting, and snazzy close-coupled looks, was a poor man's Thunderbird and as such sold well. Priced at about $2,200, the Monza cost $1,500 less than the T-Bird, and some $500 less than the Triumph TR3. Yet it combined the four seats of the Thunderbird with the agile performance of the Triumph. In 1961, Chevy offered an optional four-speed gearbox, which added to the Monza's sporty appeal.

Although Chevrolet built only about 12,000 Monzas in what was left of the 1960 model year, it built 143,000 of the 1961 versions. When a convertible was added in 1962, sales shot up past the 200,000 mark. For the really serious driver, the 150-hp turbocharged Monza Spyder was added to the line in 1962. The Spyder later evolved into the 1965 Corvair Corsa. Spyders and Corsas were rapid, good handling cars of a size and character Chevrolet had never built before. And over a bit of winding road, a well-driven Monza Spyder could give fits to an MG driver.

So, the Corvair earned sales success not as an economy car, but as a sporty, fun-to-drive compact which opened up a whole new market in the early '60s. Quite naturally, the Monza was not alone in its field for long. By 1962, Chrysler had jumped into the fray with bucket-seat versions of the Plymouth Valiant and Dodge Lancer. That same year also saw the Chrysler Windsor replaced by the "non-letter" 300 series. Priced at around $3,500, the 300 model sold well by

1962 Dodge Lancer GT

1962 Buick Special Skylark

1962 Oldsmobile Cutlass Jetfire

1961 Pontiac Tempest LeMans

offering a conventional engine combined with the styling, bucket seats, and center console of the "letter-series" 300s.

But public interest and sales battles centered mainly on the sporty compact. Rival GM divisions were quick to follow the Monza's lead with flashy machines like the

Buick Special Skylark, Pontiac Tempest LeMans, and Oldsmobile F-85 Cutlass. Studebaker chimed in with the Lark Daytona in 1963. The Daytona offered the obligatory bucket seats, plus complete instrumentation, and options like disc brakes, four-speed gearbox, a sunroof, and performance V-8s of up to 300 hp.

Ford Motor Company was not about to be left out of this money-making picture. Its first answer to the Corvair Monza was the Falcon Futura coupe, which arrived in the spring of 1961. Like the Monza, the Futura had bucket seats and a deluxe interior and it remained in production unchanged through 1963. A more exciting Futura was the Sprint, first offered in the spring of 1963 as a convertible or hardtop. The Sprint was powered by what would turn out to be a significant

1962 Ford Falcon Futura

1963 Ford Falcon Futura Sprint

1963 Mercury Comet S-22

new engine—Ford's small-block 260 cubic-inch V-8 with 164 horsepower. When this powerful, efficient engine was coupled to an optional four-speed gearbox, the Sprint was a truly exciting, vivid performer. And, it had all the visible features that symbolized performance in the '60s: bucket seats, consoles, and a full set of special instruments including a 6000-rpm tachometer.

Sprints continued in production through the first Falcon restyle of 1964, and the second restyle of 1966. By then, Ford had increased displacement of the small-block to 289 cubic inches and offered it as a Sprint option. In 1967, the "Stage 2" small-block with four-barrel carburetors offered 225 hp. Mercury's Falcon-based Comet S-22 and Comet Cyclone were similar in concept and performance to the Futura and Futura Sprint.

But anyone could see by the sales figures that the bucket-seat Falcons and Comets were not sufficiently competitive with the Corvair Monza. Whether it was because of the Corvair's novel rear engine and four-wheel independent suspension, or superior promotion by Chevrolet, buyers were not as attracted to Corvair's competition. In 1963, for example, Ford built 73,000 Futuras and S-22 Comets. In 1964, it built 118,000 of these sporty compacts. Meanwhile, Chevrolet produced a whopping 350,000 Corvair Monzas in the same two-year period. If Ford was going to catch the Monza in the sales race, it would need a brand-new product. That car, like the four-seat Thunderbird, would have to be designed from the ground up especially for the sporty compact market.

It is important to realize that, in the years immediately before the Mustang's launch, Ford was in an ideal position to create such a car. A succession of able managers who had joined Ford since 1945 had turned the once-ailing company into a mighty colossus. In the early 1950's, it had overtaken Chrysler as the number-two producer. During that decade, Ford Division had actually outproduced Chevrolet on several occasions. In the early '60s, Ford experienced continually growing sales. In 1964, for example, Ford Division produced nearly 1.8 million cars, a figure exceeded only by 1923 at that time.

The decision to launch a new, sporty, and personal—but by no means limited-edition—car occurred in 1961. Yet this car could not have been developed without the consistant sales success of the regular product line. Had the 1961-64 Fords sold poorly—or had the company created another Edsel—we might not have seen the Mustang until 1968 or 1969, if then.

The reason Ford Division cars sold well in the early '60s is due largely to its general manager of that period, the man who was McNamara's replacement. McNamara had been an astute leader, but he was not an automobile man. His successor combined all of McNamara's business sense, together with an enthusiast's appreciation of automobile design and the drive of a hard-working salesman. With a father like Lee Iacocca, the Mustang could hardly be anything less than a stunning success.

False Starts: Mustang I and XT~Bird

Lee Iacocca's father, Nicola, emigrated to America at the age of 12 from southern Italy. As a teenager, he had scraped together enough cash to buy a second-hand Model T, which he rented out from time to time to acquaintances in and around Allentown, Pennsylvania. Within eight years, Nicola's rental business had blossomed to 33 cars, most of them Fords. Soon, the elder Iacocca had expanded and branched out into real estate. Before the Depression, the family's holdings reached a net worth of over a million dollars—a fortune they even managed to keep largely intact through those hard times.

Wrote *Time* magazine in a 1964 cover story on Nicola's son Lee at the time of the Mustang's introduction: "Lee Iacocca never wavered from early youth in his desire to go into the auto business—with Ford. For him, it was something like wanting to join the priesthood. 'I suppose it was partly because my father had always been greatly interested in automobiles,' he says, 'and because I was influenced by family friends who were Ford dealers.' "

Lee Iacocca breezed through high school with excellent grades, received his bachelor's degree from Lehigh University, and then got a master's degree in mechanical engineering from Princeton on a scholarship. Next, he whizzed through a scheduled 18-month Ford marketing course in only half that time, and soon afterward, found himself with an offer to become a Ford transmission engineer. Iacocca decided that was not for him, so instead he took a job in a tiny Ford sales outpost in Pennsylvania. He did exceedingly well and began climbing the ladders of various Ford regional sales offices. In 1956, he came to the attention of Robert F. McNamara, who had borrowed a sales scheme that Iacocca had dreamed up in Pennsylvania. McNamara applied it to the whole country. This was the "$56 a month for a 1956 Ford" plan, and it worked. McNamara said later that it helped sell an additional 72,000 of the 1956 models. From there, promotions came thick and fast as the cigar-puffing Iacocca boosted sales of any car or truck he ever touched, even though Ford often didn't build them the way Iacocca would have liked.

Iacocca had a habit of keeping little black books which he used to chart and plan his career. At one point, he wrote in one of these books that by age 35 he intended to become a Ford vice-president. Those black books had already become the topic of dinner conversations all over Dearborn. One of the stories told about Iacocca at the time concerned an incident where he had run into flak from subordinates who resented so young a man telling them what to do. As the story goes, he passed out little black books, and asked members of his staff to write down what each of them expected to accomplish over the next few years, and in what order of importance. Then, every three months, Iacocca would grade his staff against their own self-imposed goals. When some of the older men groused about this rating method, he told them, "Get with it. You're being observed. Guys who don't get with it don't play on the club after awhile." One staffer snuffled, "He really knows how to whipsaw his men with that notebook."

Iacocca's 35th birthday came and went without a vice-presidency. Later he told a *Newsweek* reporter that he was so disappointed he thought to himself, "Hell, that's the end." But 18 days after that 35th birthday, Henry Ford II called Iacocca into his office and asked him if he'd like to be a Ford Division vice-president. One year after that, in 1960, Iacocca had taken McNamara's place as Ford Division general manager.

The Mustang, too, was one of those entries in Iacocca's personal black book. It was an idea that sprang from his hunch that there must be a market out there looking for a car. That hunch was backed up by several important facts. For one thing, people were still writing to Ford, begging the company to revive the original two-seat Thunderbird: They missed its "personal" character. Meanwhile, Chevrolet had found an unexpected mini-bonanza with the Corvair Monza. Sales of imported sports cars, like Jaguar, MG, Triumph, and Austin-Healey, were up to a brisk 80,000 units a year despite the fairly high prices of these cars. Also relatively expensive, but much admired and talked about, were the Chevrolet Corvette and the Studebaker Avanti. Iacocca reasoned that the flashiness and performance of costlier cars like these could be stuffed into an inexpensive car for the masses.

So here was the glint of a trend, and Iacocca had scribbled it down in his black book. He was thinking of the sort of car he himself might want—a young man's car. But the idea was still pretty hazy in early 1961. The car didn't yet have a name, of course. Nor was it defined as having two seats or four seats; a front, rear, or center engine location; or a metal or fiberglass body. All those decisions would come later.

For the moment, Iacocca was still trying to change the somewhat lackluster image Ford Division had acquired under McNamara. McNamara had been a good administrator: He left Ford Division in beautiful financial shape. But his steadfast refusal to build anything—no matter how exciting—if it didn't sell in large volume had cost Ford the sporty image it had begun to acquire with the two-seat Thunderbird. *Time* commented that McNamara's cars were "...like McNamara himself, (with) rimless glasses and hair parted in the middle."

When Iacocca took over as Ford general manager, he started to spruce up the division's various model lines. He arrived too late to do much about the 1961-62 models, which were already approved. But he was able to jazz up the mid-year 1963½ offerings considerably. It was Iacocca who dropped the first V-8 into the Falcon to create the Futura Sprint, put fastback roofs on some of the big Ford models, and plunged the division back into auto racing in a big way. With the blessing of Henry Ford II, the company reentered NASCAR competition and was very successful on the big southern tracks. By 1965, Ford had also won Sebring and Indianapolis, and had almost won Le Mans. It was all part of Iacocca's "thinking young."

Iacocca first broached the subject of a youth-oriented sporty car at a 1961 meeting of the Fairlane Group, an informal eight-man committee composed of top Ford executives plus members of the Ford Division ad agency. The Fairlane Group got its name from the Fairlane Inn Motel on Michigan Avenue in Dearborn where its meetings were held each week. The group decided that Iacocca's idea might be worth pursuing. The project was given the code name T-5. (Much later, production 1965 Mustangs were sold in Germany under the designation T-5.)

Two additional groups now became involved in T-5: market research, under the direction of Ford Marketing manager Chase Morsey, Jr.; and a team of young Ford engineers and designers headed by Donald N. Frey, who at that time was Iacocca's product planning manager at Ford Division. The reason for bringing in market research, of course, was either to prove or disprove Iacocca's hunch. Product planning's role was to come up with a car to fill the market void—if indeed there was one.

Morsey's research came up with some very encouraging conclusions. First, members of the postwar baby boom were just reaching car-buying age in 1960. Further, the number of young people aged 15-29 would increase by about 40 percent between 1960 and 1970, while the population of the 30-39 age bracket would actually decrease by nine percent during that decade.

Second, Morsey expected buyers between 18 and 34 to account for more than half the projected increase in new car sales from 1960 through 1970. Third, research showed that car styling in the '60s would need to reflect the preferences and tastes of this new group of younger buyers, not the older generations. Young people had clear ideas about styling and performance. The study concluded: ". . . 36 percent of all persons under 25 liked the 'four on the floor' feature. Among those over 25, only nine percent wanted to shift gears. Bucket seats were a favorite feature among 35 percent of young people, as against 13 percent in the older groups. . ." Fourth, buyers were becoming more educated, more sophisticated, and more willing to spend cash for what the study termed "image extensions." And finally, more families had more money. The number of families with incomes of $10,000 and up was expected to rise 156 percent between 1960 and 1975. Thus, more families were able to afford second (and even third or fourth) cars. Women and teenagers especially were the family members who most wanted cars of their own.

So, a potential and sizeable market definitely did exist. It was a young, affluent group, big enough to create substantial demand for the right kind of new car—something distinctive and sporty, but not too expensive. The question faced by the T-5 product planners was what should the T-5 be?

One of the very first alternatives considered was the Mustang I, a two-seat sports car—a revival of the original Thunderbird concept. Aimed more at the Triumph-MG market rather than the Corvette-Jaguar field, such a car might be the market-filler Morsey had identified.

The Mustang I was the product of an inspired triumvirate: an engineer, a stylist, and a product planner. The engineer was Herb Misch, who came to Dearborn from Packard when former Studebaker-Packard president James Nance was named to head the Edsel Division. The stylist was Gene Bordinat. The product planner was Roy Lunn, formerly of Aston Martin, and later a member of Ford's Product Study Vehicles Department. Lunn was the man who laid out the Mustang I's basic design objectives.

Because it seemed necessary to start from the ground up, the design of the Mustang I was carefully considered. As a challenger to the Triumph and MG, the car was planned for a wheelbase of 85 to 90 inches, and an engine of 1.5 to 2.0 liters, mounted centrally in a multi-tubular frame covered by an aluminum body. Since it was impossible to build a prototype body very rapidly in Detroit, Ford contacted a special body builder in Los Angeles, Trautman and Barnes. T&B built the frame out of one-inch steel tubing. The stressed-skin body was built from aluminum panels only .06-inch thick, but was given added rigidity by means of an integral roll bar and seat structure. Being fixed, the seat did not adjust but the pedals and steering wheel did. The pedals were mounted on a sliding box-member which allowed pedal position to be adjusted to any driver.

Ford engineer Herb Misch (left) and styling chief Gene Bordinat (right) inspect Mustang I in 1962.

Lunn and Misch designed the car's four-wheel independent suspension, which was an important innovation for Detroit, land of the solid rear axle. The car's rear suspension used upper wishbones and lower triangulated arms coupled to radius rods. The suspension's attachment points were widely spaced so that stress would be evenly distributed throughout the car's structure. Up front were wishbones, splayed coil springs, and Monroe telescopic shocks. All shocks and springs were adjustable for ride height and firmness. Steering was by a rack-and-pinion unit similar to the one used for the Ford Cardinal prototype, which later evolved into Germany's production Taunus 12M. The steering was geared to provide just 2.9 turns lock-to-lock and a turning circle of 30 feet.

The Mustang I's engine was placed behind the cockpit ahead of the rear wheels. Derived from the Cardinal engine, it was a 60-degree V-4 displacing 1927 cc (90 x 60 mm bore and stroke). It produced 90 hp at 6500 rpm and breathed through a small, single-throat Solex carburetor. (A competition version of this power unit had two twin-throat sidedraft Weber carbs and a cross-over manifold, and produced over 100 hp.)

Bolted to the engine was a four-speed transaxle (also derived from the Cardinal), with a cable-operated gearchange mechanism. A 7½-inch diameter clutch with special linings, adapted from the English Ford Consul, was used. Although the transmission ratios weren't particularly close (4.02, 2.53, 1.48, 1.00), the 3.30:1 rear axle ratio made them suitable for the V-4.

The Mustang I followed accepted production sports car practice in having disc brakes at the front and drums at the rear. The parking brake operated on the rear drums and would be less expensive for mass production than one working on rear discs. The front

Mustang I cockpit was functional but stark.

Bucket seats did not adjust but pedals did.

brakes were designed to take about 80 percent of the total braking load, and were 9½-inch Girling units borrowed from the English Ford 109E. The 13-inch magnesium wheels were built for Ford by Lotus of England, and shod with Pirelli radial-ply tires.

Dimensionally, the Mustang I measured 154 inches in overall length, had a 90-inch wheelbase, and its track was 48 inches front, 49 inches rear. The car's lightweight construction resulted in an overall weight of less than 1,200 pounds, which allowed the V-4 engine to deliver astounding performance. The Mustang I's top speed was approximately 115 mph. Because of the car's low nose there was minimal space for a radiator and ductwork at the front, so the engine was cooled by two centrally located, diagonally mounted radiators, one per side, each equipped with a thermostatically-controlled fan. The 13-gallon aluminum-alloy fuel tank had a quick-fill neck, and the spare tire was stored in the front compartment.

Mustang I styling went from sketch to approved clay model in just 21 days under the direction of Gene Bordinat. Thanks to Lunn, the car met Federacion Internationale d'Automobile (FIA) and Sports Car Club of America (SCCA) regulations for race cars. Even the

roll bar was SCCA-legal. So was the racing windshield, although that would obviously have to be replaced by a full windshield if the car went into mass production. The Mustang I had no soft top, but a light folding hardtop was designed for possible production and would have attached to the header of a normal windshield. Concern for good aerodynamics dictated the use of retracting headlights and even a folding front license plate mount. The car was low—less than 40 inches high—though it cleared the ground by nearly five inches.

Interior styling was another rush job by Ford's studio, but it was nicely executed. The instrument panel used a five-pod arrangement which housed the fuel gauge, speedometer, tachometer, ammeter and water temperature gauges. Ignition and light switches were mounted to the left in an angled extension of the driver's armrest, and a passenger grab handle hung from the dashboard itself on the right. The choke and horn button were mounted on the central console alongside the shift lever and handbrake. A small rubber mat covered the center part of the floor. In appearance, the cockpit was starkly functional but practical, in keeping with the design goal of low production costs.

The Mustang I was first displayed at the United States Grand Prix at Watkins Glen in October 1962, where it was driven around the circuit to the cheers of fans by racing driver Dan Gurney. Later, *Car and Driver* magazine tested the 90-hp version, and found that Mustang I was as fast as Ford claimed. Acceleration from 0 to 60 mph took about 10 seconds, yet fuel economy was as high as 30 miles per gallon. The handling was excellent, according to *Car and Driver:* "It reminds us of the first two-seat 1100 cc Coventry Climax-engined Cooper more than any other car, and the Mustang seemed more forgiving. It can be braked well into a turn, and with power on its stability is striking." The magazine also praised the beautifully precise rack-and-pinion steering. But the editors felt body modifications would be needed to provide adequate luggage space. There wasn't any up front, because the space there was occupied by the spare tire, fuel tank, and various hydraulic reservoirs. The retractable lights, too, would need to have electric servo motors: On the prototype the driver had to get out and hand-crank them into position.

Innovative and exciting though it was, the Mustang I was a false start. While Ford engineers and stylists, Dan Gurney, and the sports car people raved, Iacocca watched public reaction carefully and shrugged. "All the buffs said, 'Hey what a car! It'll be the best car ever built,' " Iacocca said later. "But when I looked at the guys saying it—the offbeat crowd, the real buffs—I said, 'That's sure not the car we want to build, because it can't be a volume car. It's too far out.' "

Iacocca's conclusion may have been influenced by a prior decision on the Cardinal project. Cost estimates had indicated the subcompact Cardinal, if sold in the U.S., would sell in a very competitive market sector. Iacocca had already decided to build the Cardinal in Europe as a German Taunus, but not in the United

From bottom: Mustang I, II, '65 model, and '65 GT-350.

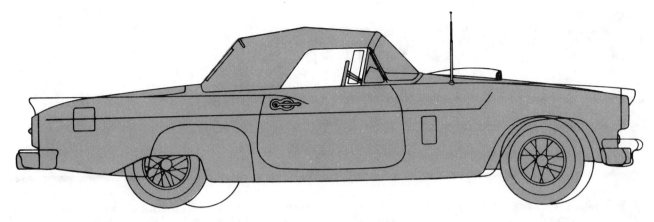

Budd's XT-Bird proposal (shaded area) used most of the original 1957 body structure.

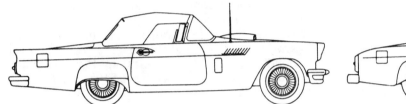

Ford had been asked to revive two-seat Thunderbird.

Falcon-based XT-Bird had updated '57 styling.

States. The Mustang I, which shared most of its major mechanical components with the Cardinal, would have been economically feasible only if Ford had planned to build the Cardinal in the U.S. as well. Without domestic production of the Cardinal, tooling costs for the Mustang I would have been prohibitive for a specialty car that Iacocca realized just wouldn't appeal to that many people.

Similar drawbacks plagued another early '60s proposal for a two-seater, the Falcon-based XT-Bird. This car was an exercise in production engineering conceived by the Budd Body Company, a long-established Ford supplier, at around the time the Mustang I was being developed. Budd had tooled the bodies for the original two-seat Thunderbird, and still had the dies for this design in 1961. Budd engineers concluded this tooling could be effectively utilized for a new production car combining the chassis and drivetrain of the 1961 Falcon with a modified version of the 1957 Thunderbird body.

To create the XT-Bird, Budd first removed the Falcon body from its chassis, retaining much of that car's underbody structure. Then, the 1957 T-Bird body was updated in styling by shearing off the tailfins and lowering the front fenders. Ingeniously, Budd managed to retain the original '57 Thunderbird dashboard and cowl. In deference to then-current styling, however, Budd reshaped the severe dog leg of the '57 car's wraparound windshield so that the A-pillar was less angled and front quarter vents were added. The XT-Bird, like the original '57 model, had a folding soft top which disappeared into a well ahead of the decklid. But unlike the two-seat Thunderbird, Budd's proposed car also had a small rear jump seat, which could hold children, or could be folded down to form a luggage platform. The prototype body was made of steel. Budd estimated the finished production car could retail for about $2,800.

Budd executives went out of their way to interest Ford management in the idea because they knew Iacocca was looking for a new image-builder. They pointed out the extraordinarily high resale value of 1955-57 Thunderbirds, and suggested this indicated a strong, unmet buyer demand for an updated version of that car. "The total tool, jig, and fixture costs for production of the XT-Bird would not exceed $1.5 million," Budd wrote. "We could ship the entire body-in-white for the XT-Bird to the Ford Motor Company for a total unit cost of between $350 and $400 . . . We believe that we could be shipping complete bodies in white for this car six months from the day you authorize us to start the job."

In the end, though, the XT-Bird remained only wishful thinking on the part of Budd and certain sports-car-minded product planners at Ford Division. Lack of full four-passenger capacity was the XT-Bird's main limitation, though its rather dumpy lines didn't set many hearts pounding either. Besides, Ford's own styling studio had far better ideas to offer, and at that time there were literally hundreds of proposals for Iacocca's car kicking around. Shortly, one of these would become the genesis of the first production Mustang.

On Designing a Legend

Neither the Mustang I nor the XT-Bird prototypes really appealed to the Fairlane Group. The executives also passed over two other two-seater designs—an open racer called Median, and a sports model called Mina. But by 1962, dozens of four-seat packages were also in the design stage. Some were mere paper renderings; others were quarter-scale and full-size clay models.

The Fairlane Group reviewed these cars and asked that one proposal—a four-seater dubbed "median sports car"—be worked up into coupe and convertible body styles. Its styling captured, they felt, some of the two-seat Thunderbird's personal flavor. In addition to a four-seat package, the median sports car was mocked up as a two-seater, as a two-plus-two with jump seats, and as a two-plus-two with a set of cramped rear bucket seats.

The median sports car led to a second generation of styling studies called Avventura. There were 12 different clay models in the Avventura series, one of which became what was called the Allegro X-car, first shown publicly in August 1963. Actually, there were 13 Allegros, each differing slightly in dimensions and interior packaging. Ford as much as admitted that the Allegro would never be produced by labeling it a "styling experimental car."

The Allegro was built on a 99-inch wheelbase, stood 50 inches high, and was 63½ inches wide with a 170-inch length. Its power unit was the 144 cubic-inch Falcon overhead-valve six. The drivetrain layout was conventional: a front-mounted engine and manual transmission behind it, connected by a driveshaft to a live rear axle with universal joint. Ford was now leaning towards a drivetrain based on one of its American-made production cars, though the company stated the Allegro "could accommodate the 170 cubic-inch (Falcon) six or the 1200cc or 1500cc V-4s of the (German Ford) Taunus with its front-wheel drive." Had the V-4 and fwd arrangement been used, noted *Road & Track*, "it would seem that there is space for four passengers without major body alterations, and the width of the door (for rear seat entrance) bears this out."

Like the Mustang I, the Allegro's seats were permanently fixed and the pedals were adjustable to fit the driver. The steering wheel was adjustable up and down. It also swung out of the way, like that of contemporary production Thunderbirds; a "memory button" allowed the wheel to be returned to a pre-set position once the driver was seated in the cockpit. The Allegro also featured retractable seatbelts—certainly a portent of the future. Because the seats were fixed structural members of the body, the seatbelt housings were attached directly to them, a touch which showed the influence of aircraft design practice. The Allegro and its many variations occupied the attention of Ford management for about a year, until mid-summer, 1962.

By this time, though, the Allegro theme had been worked over so much it was becoming stale. Eugene Bordinat, Donald Frey, Lee Iacocca, Henry Ford II, and their associates decided in August, 1962, to start over with a new series of clays. The basic package was determined and four Ford styling teams were invited to submit competing design proposals to fit the specifications. The package called for a target retail price of $2,500; a 2,500-pound curb weight; a 180-inch maximum overall length; four bucket seats; floorshift; and the use of mostly Falcon mechanical components. The car's character was to be "sporty, personal and tight." Finally, Ford tossed in a marketing brainstorm, probably the key to the whole concept of what would become the Mustang—a long, long option list that would let a buyer tailor the car for economy, luxury, performance, or any combination of these.

The four styling studios went to work. These were the Ford Division studio, the Lincoln-Mercury studio, Corporate Projects, and Advanced Design. All, of course, worked under Gene Bordinat, and he gave them just two weeks to come up with suitable scale

This Allegro prototype was one of 13 in all.

clays. The four groups produced a total of seven clays, and on August 16th, these were arranged side-by-side in the Ford Design Center courtyard. Of the seven, one leaped out from the rest. "It was the only one in the courtyard that seemed to be moving," Iacocca said later, and Henry Ford II agreed with his view.

That particular proposal was created by the Ford Division studio under Joe Oros, who later became executive director of Ford and Lincoln-Mercury design. Members of the Oros team included Gail Halderman, studio manager, and David Ash, executive designer. The Oros group had gathered to talk about the assignment at length, before anyone even put pencil to paper. "We said what we would and wouldn't do," says Oros. "We didn't want the car to look like any other car.

It had to be unique." They talked so much, in fact, that once they started, it only took three days to draw the proposed design that so impressed Iacocca. The styling looked very much like that of the eventual production Mustang, but without a front bumper. Oros called it the Cougar, and the name was later changed to Torino (or Turino in some applications). Finally, and confusingly, it was dubbed Mustang II. Oros deliberately painted the clay white so it would stand out at the showing and increase his team's chances of winning this not-so-friendly intramural styling showdown. Judging from the reaction of Iacocca and HF II, that strategy, and the car's styling, both succeeded handsomely.

The Cougar-Torino-Mustang II was based, like the

Early Allegro clay shows T-Bird style roof.

Long hood-short deck lines were found on all Allegros.

A convertible version was planned from the start.

This design, called Stiletto, was an Allegro off-shoot.

A fastback in the Allegro series was also considered early.

Another Allegro featured fins and side sculpturing.

Stiletto study was also revised many times by 1963.

This Allegro's full-width grille resembles 1965 Ford Galaxie.

Budd XT-Bird, on the Falcon floorpan. To provide genuine four-passenger seating capacity, it used a wheelbase of 108 inches—only 1½ inches shorter than the production Falcon's. Its track was 56 inches front and rear. Overall length was 186.6 inches—a bit more than the maximum specified in the design brief. It was intended to accept Ford drivetrains up to the 289 cubic-inch, 271-hp Fairlane V-8 engine and four-speed all-synchromesh transmission.

Later, a running prototype based on the Oros car, and also called Mustang II, was built and displayed around the country. Its first showing was at Watkins

Glen before the United States Grand Prix in the autumn of 1963. Although the people who saw the car didn't realize it at the time, the Mustang II's styling was actually a sneak preview of the forthcoming Mustang. Earlier, Iacocca had indicated that if Ford was going to mass-produce any sporty car, the Mustang II had the best chance of being that car among any of the experimentals seen to date. "Our preliminary studies," he said, "indicate that a car of this type could be built in this country to sell at a price of under $3,000."

Meanwhile Joe Oros and his staff had one more fling with a two-seater—the last significant proposal for a

Torino proposal was developed from Oros clay.

Torino's rear end hints at the future Mustang.

Note Torino's styling similarity to both Mustang II and production Mustang

two-seat car before management definitely decided on the four-seat formula. This was the Cougar II, a running prototype first shown in late 1963 and early 1964. It was a sports car with exciting lines not unlike those of the Corvette Sting Ray. Though Ford didn't mention it, the Cougar II's dimensions were very close to those of the exciting AC Cobra: 90-inch wheelbase; 50½-inch track front, 52-inch rear; 66½-inch width; 48-inch height; and 168-inch overall length. The Cougar II used a 260 cubic-inch Fairlane V-8, with four-speed all-synchromesh gearbox and independent suspension at all four wheels. Said *Road & Track*: ". . . the aerodynamics look reasonably good and the performance should be excellent, especially with one of the hotter versions of the Cobra-ized Fairlane V-8."

In a move which anticipated a future Corvette design feature, Oros incorporated a removable roof section over the passenger compartment of the Cougar II. When the panel was in place the car appeared to be a closed grand touring coupe. When the panel was removed it was discovered the fixed rear roof/backlight acted as an air scoop. This apparently had some benefit for aerodynamics but also had an unexpected side effect—a blown-out rear window. Oros accordingly added a "relief panel" behind the seats which opened when pressure against the roof/backlight reached 15 pounds per square inch.

The Cougar II was certainly the closest thing to a genuine street sports car turned out by Ford designers in this period. It also had the smoothest styling of any of

these prototypes. Alas, it suffered the same problem as the Mustang I and XT-Bird before it: Ford did not expect a two-seater to sell in sufficient volume to assure a significant return on the high costs of tooling such a car. The Cougar II also did not fit Iacocca's idea for a four-passenger personal model, and its overall styling was probably too close to the Corvette's for many at Dearborn to feel comfortable.

On September 10, 1962, the original Cougar, the white clay model with which Oros had wowed the company brass a few weeks earlier, was "validated" for production engineering. At this point, and only at this point, did Ford Engineering get involved. This was unusual, because engineers were usually called in at a much earlier stage in a car's development than was the case with the Mustang. (The need to keep styling options open was probably the cause for the delay.) Said Jack J. Prendergast, executive engineer for light vehicles: "Styling kept the engineers out too long, but even so Engineering and Styling worked together very smoothly." Except for the routine compromises needed to modify a styling prototype for mass production (conventional bumpers, round headlights, a less rakish windshield angle), relatively few changes were made to the Oros design. Engineering bent over backward, in fact, to keep the car's styling intact.

The Mustang was mainly a body engineering job, because the basic chassis, engine, suspension, and driveline components it eventually used, all came from the Falcon and Fairlane. At 181.6 inches, overall length

Mustang II was first shown in Ford Styling's courtyard.

Mustang II's triple taillights became Mustang trademark.

Mustang II provided a sneak preview of the production car introduced a few months later.

was identical to the 1964 Falcon. The wheelbase, at 108 inches, remained 1.5 inches shorter than the Falcon. Some thought had been given initially to sharing some of the Mustang's sheetmetal with the Falcon, but that idea didn't last long.

According to Ford studio manager Gail Halderman, "We had to bend something like 78 Ford Motor Company in-house standards or rules in order to build this car." Halderman was referring to a rulebook used by Ford designers at that time listing specific do's and dont's for production cars. For example, the rules prohibited the radical tuck-under featured on the production Mustang's rear fenders; the minimal bumper-to-sheetmetal clearance that appeared on production models; the die-cast bezel in front of the headlights; and the degree of roll-under for the front bumper pan used on the final car. Where Engineering couldn't make structural pieces fit Styling's lines and curves (as in the case of the front pan, where there was no room for bumper bracing), the car's original design was revised as little as possible.

With the many optional engines and different horsepower ratings contemplated, it was essential to have a rigid base. Prendergast recalled, "The platform-type frame, evolved from previous light-car experience, was designed to be really in the middle. All the various chassis components were attached to the underside, and all the body components were installed topside." Heavy box-section side rails with five welded-in crossmembers formed the base. The convertible used heavier-gauge steel and extra reinforcements in the rocker areas. The frames of the first coupes were so stiff they actually resonated vibrations. Accordingly, the coupe chassis was softened slightly. Prendergast pointed out that at the time the Mustang was being readied for production, Engineering had learned quite a bit about noise, vibration, and harshness through experience with the Falcon and Comet. As a result, the solutions for some engineering problems on the Mustang, such as choice of suspension components, were much better than on those earlier cars. The Mustang's suspension, in fact, drew heavily on components from the later Falcon Sprint/Comet Caliente/ Fairlane series cars. A running change made to the 1964 versions of these cars anticipated the Mustang's arrival. Because of the Mustang's low hoodline, engineers lowered the air cleaner and countersunk the radiator filler cap on all Falcons, Comets, and Fairlanes—cars with which the Mustang would share these components. In a similar way, all mechanical parts for the Mustang were in production and catalogued several months before the actual production car debuted.

Meanwhile, there was still the problem of naming the new car. Although the name "Mustang" had been seriously considered early on, as shown by the Mustang I two-seater, it took some time before this designation prevailed. Different Ford departments had applied a variety of working titles to the project, including Allegro, Avventura, Cougar, Turino and Torino, as well as Mustang. Henry Ford II favored

"T-Bird II" or "Thunderbird II." Surprisingly, Iacocca had no strong preferences.

To research a name, John Conley, from Ford's ad agency, went to the Detroit Public Library to see what he could come up with. It was Conley who had earlier combed through lists of birds to discover the name Falcon which was chosen for Ford's 1960 compact. (Chrysler, he later learned, had discovered it even earlier and used it for a 1955 experimental sports car. But a friendly phone call to Chrysler from Henry Ford II netted Dearborn the rights to that name.)

This time Conley searched through names of various horses. Mustang, of course, was already on his list. But he also considered Colt, Bronco, Pinto, and Maverick. All four of these names were eventually used for cars—Colt by Dodge; Bronco, Pinto, and Maverick by Ford, of course. Mustang, however, was the clear choice at this time for the new automobile. In many ways it was a natural. It connoted cowboys, prairies, movie adventures, the romantic West. It was easy to spell and easy to remember. As one Ford ad man said, "It had the excitement of the wide-open spaces, and it was American as all hell." A symbol for the wild, free-spirited horse of the Western plains was thus carved out of mahogany and became the now-familiar emblem that graced the grille of the first production prototype.

Target date for the Mustang's introduction as a 1965 model was April 17, 1964. The place was to be the New York World's Fair, which opened that day. Of course, the public's appetite had been whetted for years before that by a succession of exciting Ford sports show cars, including the Mustang I and II, the Allegro, and the Cougar II. But Ford decided to whet it some more by "accidentally" baiting the press. On March 11th, Henry Ford's 20-year-old nephew, Walter Buhl Ford III, just happened to drive a black preproduction Mustang convertible to lunch in downtown Detroit. Fred Olmsted, auto editor for the Detroit *Free Press,* spotted it in a parking lot and called photographer Ray Glonka to hurry on over to snap a shot. Glonka's picture was picked up by *Newsweek* and a number of other publications, giving a national audience its first glimpse of the new Mustang. If anything, those sneak photos only heightened the public's desire to see the car in full.

Time magazine had made a deal with Ford which allowed the news weekly to take pictures of the Mustang as it was being developed. *Time* photographer J. Edward Bailey had been with Oros and Bordinat almost since the beginning of the Mustang II clay, and the magazine in return had promised not to publish anything about the new car until introduction day. *Time* kept its promise, but despite its hopes for an exclusive, *Newsweek* ran a simultaneous cover story on Iacocca and his baby's birth the same week as *Time's.* It was a rare trick that Ford publicists had pulled. In a barrage of media coverage, *Life, Look, Esquire, U.S. News & World Report*, the *Wall Street Journal,* and most business and automotive publications all carried big articles on the Mustang just days before the car went on sale. On the evening of April 16th, Ford bought the 9 pm time slot on all three major TV networks and an estimated 29 million viewers saw the Mustang's unveiling without leaving their living rooms. The next morning, 2,600 major newspapers carried announcement ads and articles.

Meanwhile, some 150 auto editors had been invited as Ford's guests to the World's Fair and some sumptuous wining and dining. The next day, they were set loose in a herd of Mustangs for a drive from New York to Detroit. "These were virtually hand-built cars," recalls one Ford information officer, "and anything could have happened. Some of the reporters hot-dogged these cars the whole way, and we were just praying they wouldn't crash or fall apart. Luckily everyone made it, but it was pure luck." The luck paid off in glowing reports in the following weeks.

Mustangs were soon put on display in airport terminals, Holiday Inn lobbies, and dealer showrooms across the country. Everywhere, the car's price ($2,368 f.o.b. Detroit for the coupe) was boldly advertised. Crowd reaction was tremendous. One San Francisco trucker was staring so hard at a Mustang sitting in a dealer's showroom that he drove right in through the window. A Chicago dealer had to lock his doors to keep people from crowding in and crushing his cars—and each other. A Pittsburgh dealer made the mistake of hoisting his only Mustang up on a lube rack: The crowds pressed in so thick and fast to get a look at the car he couldn't get it down until supper time. At one eastern dealership, where 15 customers wanted to buy the same new Mustang, the car was finally auctioned off. The winning bidder insisted on sleeping in his car to be sure it wasn't sold out from under him before his check cleared the next morning.

It was the same story all over the country: Dealers simply couldn't get Mustangs fast enough. All the early cars were sold at or above retail, and with very unliberal trade-in allowances. Long before the introduction date, Ford had projected first year sales of 100,000 cars. As the World's Fair approached, Iacocca upped the estimate to 240,000 and switched over assembly facilities at Ford's San Jose, California, plant to Mustang production. Iacocca had been conservative: It took only four months to sell 100,000 Mustangs. During the 1965 model run (April, 1964, through December, 1965) a total of 680,992 cars had been sold. This figure set an all-time industry record for first-year sales. By March, 1966, the one-millionth Mustang had rolled off the line. This sales record is even more impressive in view of the limited body styles available: Only two, the coupe and the convertible, were offered until September, 1964, when a fastback was added to the line.

A legend had been created literally overnight. But if the Mustang was an instant hit it was because years of effort and planning had been put into its concept and design. The planning had paid off—the Mustang was a success because it proved to be right for a vast, hitherto untapped market. As a sports car, or a sporty car, it was deficient in some ways. Yet in other ways, it was better than anyone expected. But by almost any yardstick, the production Mustang was certainly the start of a Detroit revolution: The stampede was on.

This, of course, is how the first Mustang eventually turned out in April, 1964.

The First Revolution: 1965

The reaction of most automotive experts to the new Mustang was qualified enthusiasm. The early mixed reviews stemmed partly from the nature of the car itself: Underneath that striking new shape, the Mustang was little more than just another Detroit compact. However, most critics were willing to forgive the Mustang for having such humble origins because performance and handling options were available to turn this warmed-over compact into a competent grand tourer. In fact, Ford's vast option list covered virtually every mechanical and physical aspect of the car.

There really was no such thing as a typical Mustang. Perhaps more than with any car before it, the character of any particular Mustang depended on how the car was equipped. This chameleon-like ability to take on so many different personalities also accounts for the wide range of reactions to the car when it was first announced. So, the Mustang's options are worth mentioning, if only to indicate their variety and their importance in the car's appeal to such a wide range of customers. It was this broad appeal that made the Mustang such a resounding sales success.

Standard equipment on the "1964½" Mustang included the 170-cid Falcon six, a three-speed manual floorshift transmission, full wheel covers, padded dash, bucket seats, and carpeting. From there, the customer could personalize the car in any number of ways.

Typical options included: Cruise-O-Matic transmission, four-speed manual transmission, or overdrive three-speed transmission; a choice of three different V-8s; limited-slip differential; Rally-Pac gauges (tachometer and clock); special handling package; power brakes; disc brakes (from late 1965 on); power steering; air conditioning (except on "Hi-Performance" 271-hp V-8s); console; deluxe steering wheel; vinyl roof covering; pushbutton radio with antenna; knock-off-style wheel covers; 14-inch styled steel wheels; and whitewall tires. There were also option packages: a Visibility Group (mirrors and wipers); an Accent Group (pinstriping and rocker panel moldings); an Instrument Group (needle gauges for fuel, water, oil pressure, and amperes, plus a round speedometer); and a GT Group (disc brakes, driving lights, and special trim). The most expensive option, air conditioning, listed at only $283. Many of the more desirable extras, like the handling package ($31), front disc brakes ($58), Instrument Group ($109), and Rally-Pac ($71) were easily affordable by the average buyer. The Mustang took up the personal car theme of its forebears with an option list longer than anything Detroit had ever contemplated—or offered. For less than $3,000 any customer could order a very individual, very exciting automobile depending, of course, on whether the person was willing to wait for his specially optioned dream.

Sporty good looks and a long option list would help Mustang set sales records its first year.

One of the many options for the 1965 Mustang convertible was a power-operated top.

The '65 interior had bucket seats and full carpeting.

The name and the symbol spell success.

Mustang engine options were the key to personalizing the cars. During the long 20-month 1965 model run, powerplant offerings were shuffled slightly. For example, the original standard engine, the 170-cid Falcon six with 101 hp, was dropped after September 1964, which is considered the accepted "break" between the early "1964½" cars and the "1965" Mustangs. Its replacement was a 200-cid six with 120 hp. The 200 was an improvement on the 170, because of its higher compression, redesigned valve arrangement, and seven (instead of five) main bearings. The new six also featured an automatic choke, a short-stroke cylinder block design for longer piston and cylinder wear, hydraulic valve lifters, and an intake manifold integral with the cylinder head.

The smallest Mustang V-8 offered for the 1964½ models was the 260-cid small-block with 164 hp. Derived from the 260 was the 289-cid V-8, which produced 195 hp with two-barrel carburetor, or 210 hp with the optional four-barrel carb. A "Hi-Performance" (HP) version of the 289 four-barrel had 271 hp. After September 1964, the 260 was discontinued and a two-barrel 289 with 200 hp became the base optional V-8. Output of the four-barrel was then boosted to 225

hp, while the 271-hp HP version was left unchanged. The four-barrel 289 cost $162 extra, and the 271-hp version cost $442 extra.

These small-block V-8s were classic designs—light, efficient, and powerful. Advanced, thin-wall casting techniques made them the lightest cast-iron V-8s on the market. They featured short-stroke design; full-length, full-circle water jackets; high-turbulence, wedge-shaped combustion chambers; hydraulic valve lifters; automatic choke; and centrifugal vacuum advance distributor. The four-barrel engines achieved their extra power by increased carburetor air velocity matched to the performance curve of the engine. They also had different valve timing than the two-barrel engines, plus a higher compression ratio which demanded use of premium fuel.

The Hi-Performance 271-hp engine was the ultimate factory powerplant. It developed .95 hp per cubic inch and offered 312 foot-pounds of torque at 3400 rpm. Its design featured a high-compression cylinder head, high-lift camshaft, free-breathing air intake system, free-flow exhaust, solid valve lifters, low-restriction air cleaner, and chrome-plated valve stems. Although the 289's power seemed to be the answer to every dragster's dream, there were ways to improve the Mustang's performance even more. For about $500, a visit to your friendly Ford parts counter would buy an impressive amount of "Cobra equipment."

Cobra equipment included such items as special camshafts, heads, and intake manifolds; dual four-barrel carburetion; and even Weber carburetors. All these goodies were considered factory-stock, even though none of them were actually installed at the factory. Said *Road & Track:* "The Cobra equipment will do a fabulous job if you set it up right, and you don't have to switch basic engines. You just bolt it onto your standard V-8. Also, this equipment will now be legal in the FX classes at the dragstrip."

The $73 Cobra "cam kit" consisted of solid valve lifters and a 306-degree duration cam with .289-inch lift. The $222 "cylinder head kit" comprised two stock 271-hp heads with extra-large intake and exhaust valves, and heavy-duty valve springs and retainers. Matched pistons, combined with the cam and head kits, made up the $343 "engine performance kit." Then

there were the carburetors and manifolds. A single four-barrel carb and a big-port aluminum manifold cost $120. With dual four-barrels the manifold kit cost $243, and with triple two-barrels the price was $210. As a final touch, a dual-point centrifugal distributor was available for $50.

Exactly how much horsepower could be wrung out of a Mustang engine with Cobra equipment is uncertain. Ford tested a stock 271-hp V-8 with four-barrel carburetor on a dynamometer, and recorded only 232 hp at 5500 rpm. This was hardly the advertised 271 hp at 6000 rpm. However, Ford's engine was tested with all normal hardware installed. A stripped engine minus the ancillaries was used as the source of the advertised figure. An unstripped 289 fitted with special distributor, hot heads, triple carburetors, and special (non-Cobra) headers, recorded a dynamometer reading of 314 hp at 6500 rpm. So in terms of advertised horsepower, 350 or more might not be too much to claim for a Cobra-equipped engine. "You'll be able to feel that on the street," commented one engineer.

Ford said no to this two-seat Mustang proposal.

Two-seater has 1965 styling but shorter wheelbase.

Fastback was, for the most part, ready by late 1963.

Fastback proposal is similar to production car.

A four-speed gearbox was mandatory on the 271-hp Hi-Performance engine. The HP was also the only engine offered with optional "short" rear axle ratios suitable for drag racing (3.89:1 and 4.11:1). Standard ratios were 3.20 with the six, 2.80 for the two-barrel V-8s, 3.00 for the four-barrel V-8s, and 3.50 with the HP V-8s. It could be argued that with ratios like 2.80:1 the milder Mustangs were undergeared. But Ford couldn't ignore customers who preferred the economy and smooth highway cruising of cars so equipped.

Front disc brakes were offered late in the 1965 model year as a $58 extra—and were well worth the money. Built by Kelsey-Hayes, they were cast-iron units of one-piece construction. The disc diameter was 9.5 inches. A radial rib separated the two braking surfaces, and each brake pad was actuated by two cylinders. Discs were valuable options because the Mustang's front drum brakes were not noted for their fade resistance.

The fastback body style, which Ford added to the line in the autumn of 1964, was called the "2+2" in the brochures. Rear legroom was scanty in this model—even less than in the other models. Unlike the coupe or convertible, however, the fastback's rear seat folded down, and a partition between it and the trunk dropped forward. When the seat and partition were lowered, a long platform was created which could accommodate items like skis or fishing rods. The sleek-looking fastback lacked the rear quarter windows of the other body styles. Instead, its rear roof pillars had little air vents, which allegedly provided flow-through ventilation.

The long-hood, short-deck appearance of the Mustang was its most important styling characteristic. It dictated the shape of what came to be known, in Mustang's honor, as the "ponycar;" in other words, a personal car with sporty characteristics. Competitors reacted as quickly as they could with cars of their own that followed the new theme, but it took time. It was not until 1967 that Chevrolet and Pontiac released the Camaro and Firebird. Ford's sister division, Lincoln-Mercury, took two years to introduce the Mustang-

A fold-down back seat was a fastback feature.

With back seat up, fastback had little trunk room.

The good-looking Mustang fastback was added to the line for the 1965 model year.

1965 Mustang hardtop

1965 Mustang "2+2" fastback

based 1967 Cougar. American Motors moved fairly rapidly by offering its Javelin ponycar for 1968. Chrysler, on the other hand, wasn't really in the running with a true ponycar until the Barracuda/Challenger.

Although the Mustang was certainly attractive, it was not an exotic or earth-shaking design. Despite its generally clean lines, the Mustang's makeup still showed traces of gingerbread. The fender "scoops" ahead of the rear-wheel openings were not functional; the shallow, high-set grille looked awkward; and detail execution around the headlights and the rear of the body was not faultless. Space utilization, given the car's 108-inch wheelbase, was marginal. Mustangs

were never comfortable for four passengers on a long trip, and their trunk space was as limited as their rear legroom. Poor space utilization was a characteristic of all the ponycars. Eventually this led to their declining popularity in the '70s as buyers became more attuned to space-efficient engineering from Europe and Japan.

Sports car magazines had more specific condemnations of the Mustang. *Road & Track,* in particular, was not happy with the car's driving position. Among the magazine's criticisms were: a deep-dish steering wheel set too close to the driver's chest; too little leg space between the clutch and the nearest interfering object (the turn indicator lever); sparse standard

The 1965 Mustang offered options for everyone in fastback, convertible, and hardtop.

instrumentation, and bucket seats that were only marginally effective in holding the occupants in place. The Mustang's low list price, R&T decided, was responsible for such lapses. But the editors admitted that the car was carpeted, trimmed, and finished "in a manner that many European sports/touring cars would do well to emulate."

Mustangs with the standard suspension were anything but grand touring cars. "The ride is wallowy, there's a tendency for the car to float when being driven at touring speeds, and the 'porpoise' factor is high on an undulating surface," R&T noted. "There's just nothing different about it in this respect...there seems little excuse for such frankly sloppy suspension on any car with the sporting characteristics which have been claimed for the Mustang." In straight-line performance, R&T's 210-hp four-speed car did about what the editors expected: 0-to-60 mph took nine seconds; the standing quarter-mile was reached in 16.5 seconds at 80 mph; top speed was 110 mph. Fuel consumption was 14 to 18 miles per gallon. Road & Track applauded the car's good looks and low price, but regretted that it was otherwise little different from "the typical American sedan."

Once Road & Track laid hands on an optioned Mustang, however, its opinion of the car changed dramatically. The test car, a 271-hp Hi-Performance version, delivered much improved acceleration and top speed: 0-to-60 time fell to 8.3 seconds; the quarter-mile took only 15.6 seconds at 85 mph; and top speed was 120 mph. Fuel consumption was down slightly to 13-16 mpg.

More interesting to the editors was the effect of the Mustang's optional and inexpensive handling package. This consisted of stiff springs and shocks, a large-diameter front anti-sway bar, 5.90x15 Firestone Super Sports tires, and a quicker steering ratio (3.5 turns lock-to-lock). "The effect is to eliminate the wallow we experienced with previous Mustangs, and to tie the car to the road much more firmly, so on a fast run the point of one's departure into the boondocks is delayed very considerably," R&T wrote. "There is a certain harshness to the ride at low speeds over poor surfaces, but this is a small price to pay for the great improvement in handling and roadholding." There was a marked degree of oversteer present in this car even though the 271 had 56 percent of its weight on the front wheels. But its hard suspension, R&T said, inspired more confidence in the driver.

The editors now cheered the HP Mustang as "a big step in the right direction." But they looked forward to the advent of disc brakes and independent rear suspension. Until then, R&T said, it would be "reluctantly unconquered." The discs showed up as an option within months, but irs never materialized. And Road & Track never became truly "conquered."

As an exponent of what Iacocca called "the sports car crowd, the real buffs," Road & Track was perhaps the most harsh of all the car magazines in its judgement of the Mustang. Motor Trend, a magazine whose tastes favored Detroit products, liked all ver-

Specifications

Model Year Production
(April 1964-August, 1965)

No.	Model	1965
63A	Fastback, standard	71,303
63B	Fastback, deluxe	5,776
65A	Hardtop, standard	464,828
65B	Hardtop, deluxe	22,232
65C	Hardtop, bench seats	14,905
76A	Convertible, standard	94,496
76B	Convertible, deluxe	5,338
76C	Convertible, bench seats	2,111
	TOTAL	680,989

Models	Prices/Weights
07 hardtop, 6	$2372/2445
07 hardtop, 8	2480/2720
08 convert, 6	2614/2669
08 convert, 8	2722/2904
09 fastback, 6	2589/2495
09 fastback, 8	2697/2770

General Specifications	1964½	1965
Wheelbase:	108.0	108.0
Overall length:	181.6	181.6
Overall width:	68.2	68.2
Std. Trans.:	3-speed manual	3-speed manual
Optional Trans.:	Overdrive	Overdrive
	4-speed manual	4-speed manual
	3-speed automatic	3-speed automatic

Engine Availability			1964½	1965
Type	CID	HP		
I-6	170	101	Std.	—
I-6	200	120	—	Std.
V-8	260	164	Std.	—
V-8	289	200	Opt.	Std.
V-8	289	225	Opt.	Opt.
V-8	289	271	Opt.	Opt.

sions of the new car, and the HP in particular. Their 271-hp car scored 0-to-60 in 7.6 seconds, and ran the quarter-mile in slightly less time than Road & Track's test car. It was obvious that with the right options the Mustang could be quite an automobile indeed.

An even more enthusiastic endorsement of the HP Mustang came from racing driver Dan Gurney. Writing in Popular Science, Gurney stated: "This car will run the rubber off a Triumph or MG. It has the feel of a 2 + 2 Ferrari. So what is a sports car?" Gurney's Mustang did 123 mph maximum and consistently beat a similarly equipped Corvette in quarter-mile acceleration runs.

If Ford hadn't created a true sports car in the HP Mustang, it had certainly come darn close.

Driving Impressions:
1965 Mustang and 1957 Thunderbird

In concept and market orientation, the two-seat Thunderbird and the first production Mustang have much in common. Both were created by heads-up marketing teams. Both were designed in an attempt to take advantage of what was seen as a buyer trend. The Thunderbird was born of America's passion for sports cars in the mid-1950s. The Mustang was created because of public interest in the sporty compacts of the early 1960s. Interestingly, it was a General Motors car that figured in the creation of both Ford products: The Corvette helped inspire the Thunderbird and the Corvair Monza helped spawn the Mustang. Although the similarity between the 1965 Mustang and the 1957 Thunderbird is not immediately apparent, the two compare very closely in dimensions and mechanical specifications.

But in production figures there are striking differences. During the three years two-seat Thunderbirds were offered, scarcely 50,000 were built. The Mustang sold at the rate of 1,000 a day during its first three months, and by the end of 1965, sales had passed the 400,000 mark. The two packages, though, were very much alike in one key respect: Both were aimed at the boulevard sportsman, who wanted personal "transportation" without complicated mechanical components that would be difficult and costly to repair.

The Thunderbird drifted away from its original concept with the arrival of the four-seat version in

The original Mustang (left) and the two-seat Thunderbird (right) have both become contemporary classics.

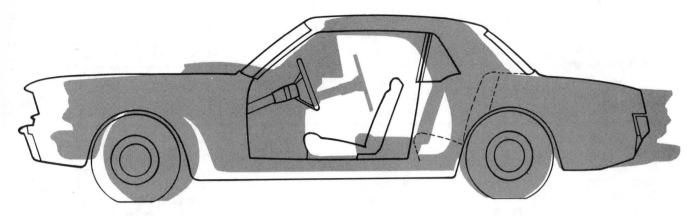

The proportions are slightly different but the T-Bird (shaded area) is dimensionally similar to the Mustang.

1958. So it makes sense to compare the last two-seat Thunderbird of 1957 with the first Mustang of 1965, even though the latter is nominally a four-seat car.

The Thunderbird we sampled for this report was strictly original inside and out—its paint, trim, and upholstery were all "factory stock." The test Mustang was also original, except that it had been repainted and some new chrome had been used to replace those pieces that were less than perfect. The Thunderbird's odometer showed 58,000 miles; the Mustang's only 32,000. Both cars were in excellent condition. The Mustang had been stored for some time and as a result had a noisy valve, but this had no effect on engine operation or performance.

The dimensional similarity between the two cars is uncanny. The Mustang does have an extra six inches of wheelbase to accommodate its rear seat, and is 4.6 inches narrower than the T-Bird. But in track, length, and height, the two cars are only fractions of an inch apart. In fact, the owner of these two cars recently bought a customized cover sized for the Thunderbird, and when he tried it on the Mustang it fit almost perfectly. Both cars have approximately the same frontal area, but the Mustang is built closer to the ground.

Engine displacements are also similar: 289 cubic inches for the Mustang, 312 for the Thunderbird. Both are V-8s, of course, having oversquare bore-and-stroke dimensions. Rear axle ratios are approximately the same and suspension layouts are identical.

When equipped with the Fordomatic transmission, as was our test car, the Thunderbird was offered with the 312-cid unit only, rated at 245 horsepower. On paper, this gave our T-Bird a slight horsepower advantage over the test Mustang GT's 225-hp 289-cid engine with four-barrel carburetor. (An even closer match for the Mustang would be a Thunderbird equipped with the 212-hp 292 cubic-inch engine and manual transmission.) Nevertheless, the results of our performance tests were interesting.

We drove the Thunderbird first. The severe dogleg caused by the wraparound windshield makes entering the car a job for a contortionist—and is an instant reminder of this faddish but impractical styling device.

Visibility is hampered somewhat by the large "A" pillar, which is ironic since wraparound windshields were claimed to improve visibility. The Thunderbird's pillar seems to hamper front and side vision more than the Mustang's, which is further forward and more conventionally angled. When the hardtop is in place there's even less headroom in the front of the T-Bird than in the *back* seat of the Mustang. There is little knee room under the big steering wheel. The full-width bench seat doesn't move back far enough for those with long legs.

Note T-Bird emblem on valve covers of 312 V-8.

Big air cleaner dominates Mustang GT's engine bay.

And the seat back doesn't recline so it's difficult to get far enough away from the wheel. The seat itself offers no lateral support but at least the backrest is set at a comfortable angle.

Despite its cramped quarters, the T-Bird is a very comfortable car to drive. There is little distortion in the windshield despite the severe wraparound glass. From the driver's seat it's obvious this is no two-seater of the MG stripe. The hood spreads out to the sides and front, and the prominent front fenders are set higher than the hood. Forward visibility is good. Sighting out the hardtop portholes is easy—they certainly do reduce that rear-quarter blind spot. The doors close with a solid clunk, and the whole car seems to impart a sense of bank-vault security.

The dashboard of the last two-seat Thunderbird could well have been the dashboard of the first Mustang. As we noted earlier in this book, Budd's proposed XT-Bird, had it been built, would have used the 1957 dash. Certainly the Bird's control panel would have worked well in the Mustang. A large hooded vinyl eyebrow shades a smart, engine-turned aluminum panel containing five gauges. In the center of the instrument cluster is a big speedometer, flanked on either side by smaller dials for fuel and temperature, engine rpm, and clock. Oil pressure and amperes are monitored only by warning lights. The tachometer is poorly located for easy reading and is therefore quite useless, although it is not really needed on an automatic-equipped car such as this. Controls for the lights, wipers, radio, and heater are all easy to reach and operate with a positive action.

The T-Bird's three-speed Fordomatic transmission offers a Drive and Low range, which are selected by means of the central floor-mounted lever with its familiar P-R-N-D-L pattern. You press a button on top of the shift knob to move the lever. The lever feels vague in its movement, though with practice it becomes easier to find the right position. The Thunderbird moves off the line fast with a hearty V-8 rumble. We timed informal 0-to-60 acceleration runs at around 10 seconds. With a curb weight close to 3,150 pounds, the 1957 Thunderbird has a good weight-to-horsepower ratio. Standing start and mid-range acceleration are excellent. The automatic transmission, although now over 20 years old, shifted cleanly and responded well to the use of Low range for engine braking and hard acceleration. There is really very little to fault in the engine or transmission of the '57 Thunderbird.

Handling is another matter. The T-Bird plows and understeers like any typical late-'50s American sedan. Enthusiastic cornering is out of the question. The steering, though power assisted, feels quite heavy and

Thunderbird styling still looks good today.

"Porthole" top was offered on the '57 T-Bird.

Grille-mounted "fog lights" distinguish Mustang GT.

Even with the top up the GT convertible has pleasing lines.

is slow to react. Even small attempts to hurry around curves are greeted by chirps of protest from the bias-ply whitewall tires. This was a bit disconcerting, since earlier we had driven a 1956 Thunderbird which displayed much better cornering response.

Undoubtedly, the Thunderbird's worst mechanical feature is its braking system. In a word, the brakes are inadequate. There's vague pedal feel, slow response to pedal pressure, and quick fade in anything more than moderate use. We noticed that Ford lists the swept area of the Thunderbird's drum brakes at only 170 square inches, compared to the 251 square inches of the Mustang's drum brakes.

All in all, our impression of the 1957 Thunderbird is that of a car that cries for suspension and braking improvements, even when judged by today's higher standards of performance. Standing still, the two-seat Thunderbird is a vision of beauty. Its design is balanced from end to end. Even the '50s styling cliches, like the tailfins, portholes, and wraparound windshield do not severely detract from its lines, which have stood the test of time very well.

The Mustang's more recent design is apparent in its better entry and egress made possible by a wide door opening and mildly raked "A" pillar. The seats are only slightly bucketed providing some, but not much, lateral support. However, they're more comfortable than the Thunderbird's bench seat, although a reclining mechanism and better side support would be appreciated. (Power seats were available for two-seat Thunderbirds, but not for 1965 Mustangs.) The windshield is higher and wider than the T-Bird's. There's little obstruction from the "A" pillars so the Mustang's outward visibility is superior to the Thunderbird's, even though you sit much lower in the Mustang. Maneuvering in tight quarters is hampered by the sheer size of the full-width hood: It is almost completely flat, and extends uninterrupted from fender to fender. With the Thunderbird, a driver has the advantage of being able to place the car by using its raised fenders and central hood scoop as aiming sights. The Mustang's vent windows are dangerously pointy and located so that when opened, they can give you a nasty poke if you're not careful.

Once seated, the driver of a standard 1965 Mustang would face a rather cheap-looking dashboard very similar to the Falcon's. But our test Mustang was a GT model which had the more informative five-dial instrument cluster. A large 140-mph speedometer is flanked by minor gauges left and right. There was no tachometer, but we didn't miss it in this automatic-equipped car. (A tach was available along with a clock as part of the optional Rally Pac which sits on the steering column under, and slightly ahead of, the dash-mounted

Gauges are clustered under hooded cowl on T-Bird.

T-Bird's single bench seat is wide but flat.

Mustang GT features five-dial instrumentation.

Mustang's front buckets are comfortable.

Odd location for spare limits T-Bird trunk space.

Like all later ponycars, Mustang's trunk is small.

instruments.) Like the Thunderbird, the Mustang has no trip odometer. Falcon knobs and switches are used for lights, wipers, and heater controls. The Mustang's steering wheel is as large as the Thunderbird's, but it's angled more comfortably and is more deeply dished.

Benefitting from nearly a decade of transmission evolution, the Mustang GT's Cruise-O-Matic three-speed automatic is more flexible than the T-Bird's Fordomatic. The Mustang's shift lever is not a "golf ball on a stick" as in the T-Bird, but rather a T-shaped handle. A lighted red arrow on the selector quadrant indicates the gear selected. The shift pattern is the same as that of the Thunderbird, except for the addition of a second drive range, and provision for manual over-ride on all three gears. On the Thunderbird, the shift from first to second occurs automatically and first gear cannot be held manually. We found the Thunderbird gear lever a little more positive in action, though neither car is good in this respect.

Pulling away from rest, the Mustang gives the sensation of great, ground-loping ability. The GT version with its tighter suspension and anti-sway bar has a firm ride compared to the standard car. On the road the suspension copes well with minor undulations, something we couldn't say for the Thunderbird. Though the GT plows a little in corners, its dominant handling trait is basically mild understeer, with controllable oversteer occurring at the limit of adhesion. With

its optional front-wheel disc brakes, the GT pulls up well from any speed. Repeated hard braking causes no perceptible fade.

Although it weighs fractionally more than the Thunderbird, the Mustang feels much heavier. It also seems tighter and more solid. This comes as a surprise because we always thought the limited-production T-Bird was very carefully assembled. Of course, the differences in mileage and age between our two test cars contribute to this impression. The Mustang showed 26,000 fewer miles and was eight years younger than the Thunderbird.

The GT's 225-hp V-8 provides a strong surge of power. Our 0-to-60 sprints were handled in less than ten seconds with the Cruise-O-Matic shifting only once under full throttle. Contemporary road tests put top speed at around 115 mph, and the performance of our test car gave little reason to doubt this. Like the Thunderbird's 312-cid engine, the Mustang 289 delivers smooth, unruffled torque for acceleration that is typical of Detroit V-8 engines. As Road & Track put it back in 1964: "We last encountered the (271-hp 289) engine in the Cobra and were unable to find any point of criticism at all, and it is equally satisfactory in the Mustang."

Unquestionably, the standard four-barrel 289 is more tractable for around-town use than the 271-hp "Hi-Performance" version, and more economical. Despite the Thunderbird's slightly higher horsepower and torque ratings, the Mustang had marginally better acceleration and top speed even though it weighed over 150 pounds more than the '57 car.

Two distinguishing exterior touches on the GT package are auxiliary fog/driving lights and rear exhaust ports. On our car, the lights were disconnected so the car could pass a state vehicle inspection. The reason, we were told, is that state codes prohibit the use of driving lights because they can't be "aimed." So, on the test car we have to regard them as more decorative than functional. The exhaust ports are more functional than practical. They look nice, but they're located so that the exhaust pipe deposits soot around the rear bumper and lower pan area. (The Thunderbird's exhaust ports are built into the outer ends of the rear bumper where they, too, are guilty of making things dirty.)

There was no chance during our test to try top-down driving in either car. Both tops are manually operated (a power-operated top was optional on the Mustang) and are easy to raise and lower. We'd judge wind protection to be good in both cars. The Thunderbird lacks the Mustang's front quarter vents, but it does have a set of glass wind wings to deflect side breezes.

In summary, both the 1957 Thunderbird and 1965 Mustang GT have many physical and mechanical similarities, but there are notable differences. Our Mustang, with its superior handling abilities, could lose the T-Bird over any sort of winding road. But ours was a Mustang GT, and the GTs had significant suspension modifications which produced much better handling than the standard car. Our Mustang also had those important front disc brakes, which enabled the car to out-stop the Thunderbird. Both cars have approximately equal, and excellent, straight-line performance. The Mustang's gas mileage is marginally better than the T-Bird's, but neither car is a fuel sipper at less than 20 mpg.

Styling is a subjective matter, although both cars rate high among industrial designers. The two-seat Thunderbird was one of the prettiest cars of its day; the long hood-short deck Mustang was equally pleasing. The Mustang's front end, like the Thunderbird's, was one of the nicer looking designs to come out of Detroit in that era. The construction quality of both cars seemed about equal, and this was a surprise. We expected the Thunderbird to be much better in this respect, despite the age and mileage differences of our two test vehicles, since it was originally a far more expensive car than the Mustang.

Both these Fords are still extremely popular today. The Thunderbird's appeal was recognized long ago, while the first Mustangs are only now becoming sought-after items. It's likely that collectors will soon be gathering Mustangs with the same enthusiasm as those who fancy early Thunderbirds. But prices of Mustangs should remain attractively reasonable for many years because so many of them were made—for every two-seat Thunderbird, 10 Mustangs were produced in 1965 alone.

For practical transportation, as well as for wowing pedestrians, both cars have much to recommend them. The Thunderbird probably has more collector appeal (and commands a higher price), because it's rarer, older, and above all, a genuine two-seater. But for those who like brisk, safe motoring in a car that handles and stops as well as it goes and looks, the Mustang GT is hard to beat. It is not a true Gran Turismo in the strict and traditional sense of the word. But it's much better in that role than the standard Mustang—and most other American cars of the mid-'60s. Like the Thunderbird before it, the Mustang GT is a satisfying, well-built car of beautiful proportions, which the collector would be proud to drive anywhere.

Specifications

	1957 Thunderbird	1965 Mustang GT
Price when new:	$4,000 approx.	$3,500 approx.
Engine type, cylinders:	ohv V-8	ohv V-8
Bore x Stroke (in.):	3.80x3.44	4.00x2.87
Displacement (cu. in.):	312	289
Compression ratio:	10.0:1	9.8:1
Horsepower @ rpm:	245 (gross) @ 4500	225 (gross) @ 4400
Transmission type/forward gears:	automatic/2	automatic/3
Final Drive ratio:	3.10:1	3.00:1
Tire size:	7.50x14	6.95x14
Steering, turns lock-to-lock:	4.0	4.0
Turning diameter (ft.):	36.5	38.0
Brake swept area (sq. in.):	170	251*
Curb weight (lbs.):	3145	3300
Weight distribution, front/rear:	55/45	56/44
Wheelbase (in.):	102	108
Overall length (in.):	181.4	181.6
Overall width (in.):	72.8	68.2
Track, front/rear (in.):	56/56	56/56
Height (in.):	52.2	51.1
Ground clearance (in.):	7.1	5.5
Suspension, front:	Independent; upper and lower A arms; coil springs; tube shocks	
Suspension, rear:	Live axle; semi-elliptic leaf springs; tube shocks	
Performance		
pounds/horsepower (gross):	12.8	16.5
acceleration, 0-60 mph (sec.):	10.5	9.8
estimated top speed (mph):	112	115

*with optional front disc brakes

Why Change a Good Thing: 1966-68

With Mustang sales roaring along as the 1966 model year approached, Ford product planners saw little reason for giving the car a major face-lift. To the casual viewer, the 1966 version seemed to be a carbon copy of the '65 model, although there were certain detail changes. Up front, the single horizontal grille bar was replaced by several thin bars. The galloping horse emblem remained, however, in its chromed rectangular frame. (Mustang GTs used a 1965-style grille which featured auxiliary driving lights mounted at the ends of a horizontal bar.) At the rear, designers restyled the fuel filler cap. Along the sides, the simulated rear wheel scoop was decorated with three windsplints. Front fender nameplates and emblems were integrated; GTs had an additional plaque on their front fenders. Finally, the stock wheel covers were redesigned.

Several more important changes were made inside the car. The cheap-looking Falcon-based standard instrument panel of 1965 was replaced by the five-gauge arrangement as used on the original Mustang GT. This included genuine needle gauges for oil pressure and amperes (a rarity among cars of the '60s). The Rally-Pac combination of tachometer and clock, mounted on the steering column, was still offered as an option.

Well before 1966, the smaller Ford six and 260-cid V-8 had been dropped from the engine lineup. Six-

Styling changes for 1966 were few: new wheel covers, grille, and windsplits for the side scoop.

Thin bars appeared for 1966 Mustang grille.

1966 Mustang GT fastback

cylinder models were also upgraded from 13- to 14-inch wheels for 1966. Engine mounts on all cars were reworked to reduce vibration. The number of Mustang engine offerings was reduced to four during this year. The base unit was the 200 cubic-inch overhead valve six. Three 289-cid V-8s were optional: the 200-hp two-barrel, 225-hp four-barrel, and 271-hp "Hi-Performance" versions. The option list was extended to include a stereo cartridge tape system and deluxe seatbelts with reminder warning light.

Sales for 1966 were not as high as in 1965 because the 1965 model year was longer than usual due to the Mustang's mid-year introduction in April, 1964. But for comparable 12-month periods, 1966 sales were superior to those of 1965 by 50,000 units. The Mustang still had no direct competition. Chevrolet was one year away from introducing its Camaro, and Corvair sales were rapidly declining. Chrysler's "glassback" Barracuda was little more than a hasty styling change to the Valiant Signet and sales were much lower than Mustang's. So Ford romped along, selling close to half a million 1966 Mustang hardtops, plus 70,000 convertibles and 35,000 fastbacks.

Ford promoted the six-cylinder Mustang rather hard in 1966. "We felt there was a need to emphasize the economy aspect at that time," one Ford executive remembers. "Also, the six-cylinder coupe was by then the only Mustang selling for less than Mr. Iacocca's original target figure." The coupe listed at $2,416, an attractive price indeed.

Though the Mustang six looked like its V-8 counterpart, it was considerably different under the skin. The wheels, upgraded to 14-inch diameter size for 1966, had only four lugs, while V-8 models had five. Sixes came with nine-inch-diameter drum brakes; V-8s had 10-inchers. The six-cylinder cars had a lighter rear axle, and a slightly narrower front track than the V-8s. Spring rates of the sixes were somewhat lower to keep the cars on an even keel—they would have looked tail-heavy if they had used the heavier V-8 suspension.

The nine-inch drum brakes, though, were quite effective—capable of stopping a Mustang from 60 mph in a slightly shorter distance than the V-8 car's discs, even though they were susceptible to fade on hard application. The Mustang six performed reasonably well for a car of its class. *Motor Trend's* automatic-equipped model accelerated from 0-to-60 mph in 14.3 seconds and averaged 20 miles per gallon of regular gas.

Most criticisms noted in Mustang road tests of the period concerned minor design flaws and one inherent problem. Deficiencies included the lack of rear-seat ashtrays and armrests, plus the absence of dashboard-level interior lights. The inherent problem was lack of interior room, a perennial drawback among all the ponycars. "Five passengers can fit," wrote *Motor Trend*, "but the fifth one usually sits on the other four's nerves." *MT* did sum up the Mustang as "safe and roadworthy, easy to handle, and fun to drive" inspite of its size limitations.

For 1967, the Chevrolet Camaro and Pontiac Fire-

1966 Mustang convertible

bird were introduced and the Plymouth Barracuda was given a major redesign. Ford thus saw a need for more Mustang improvements. The big news that year was the addition of a larger four-barrel V-8 option, the 390-cid (bore and stroke 4.05 x 3.78 inches) power-plant which developed 320 hp. This engine was standard on the Thunderbird, and offered as an option on the big Ford and intermediate Fairlane as well as the Mustang. It was first seen on the 1966 Fairlane GT. Dealers usually recommended that the 390 be teamed with the "Select-Shift" Cruise-O-Matic transmission, an automatic which could be manually held in any one of its three forward gears. The 390 engine and drivetrain options extended the total of Mustang power teams to 13. The list began as usual with the basic 200-cid 120-hp six and three-speed manual transmission, and extended through all the 289 V-8s previously available.

The 390 Mustang was certainly a potent car, but it came with a built-in front-end weight bias—58 percent of its weight was over the front wheels—so Mustang 390s understeered with merry abandon. Standard F70-14 Firestone Wide-Oval tires helped reduce the understeer somewhat but almost anybody who drove a 390 said the 289 Mustang was a far better handling car. Experts recommended that customers ordering the 390 also get the competition handling package. It consisted of stiffer springs and front stabilizer bar, Koni adjustable shocks, limited-slip differential, quick steering, and 15-inch wheels. Also available for 271-hp Mustang 289s, this option improved handling at the expense of ride.

A new dash was one of many changes for '67.

This Mustang might have been a "better idea" for '67.

certainly right in there with the top five percent of production automobiles.

Besides the potent new engine option, there were many other features which added to the 1967 Mustang's appeal. All models were restyled from the beltline down. Fastbacks got a sweeping new roofline which blended cleanly into the rear deck, and lost the slightly notched effect of the 1965-66 cars. The 1967 restyle featured a concave tail panel, a couple of extra inches added to the nose, and the loss of the gill-like impressions on either side of the grille opening. The 1967s were 2.5 inches wider and had a two-inch wider tread than the 1965-66 models. Engineers also paid attention to reducing noise and vibration by using new rubber bushings at suspension attachment points.

That change in track width was an important one because it signalled improvements in roadability. Though the track was widened mainly to provide adequate room in the engine bay for the 390 engine, it benefitted the handling of all Mustangs. The 1967's front springs were relocated above the top cross-member, as in the Fairlane. The upper A-arm pivot was also lowered and the roll center was raised, a change

The big payoff for the 390 customer was straight-line performance. Typical figures were 0-to-60 in 7.5 seconds, the standing quarter-mile in 15.5 seconds at 95 mph, and a top speed of close to 120 mph. If this wasn't the fastest car you could buy in 1967, it was

1967 Mustang got a major restyle including a long nose and deeper side sculpturing.

1967 Mustang fastback

1967 Mustang hardtop

picked up from Carrol Shelby, who used it on his GT-350s. The effect of this was to decrease understeer by holding the outside front wheel exactly perpendicular to the road when cornering. Since this change did not require the use of stiffer spring rates, the Mustang's ride did not suffer.

Against its major competition, the '67 Mustang compared quite favorably. Its economical six-cylinder engine was more miserly than those of the Barracuda or Camaro, and still provided decent performance. Mustangs were generally lighter than Camaros and Barracudas, which benefitted the Ford's performance and fuel economy. Mustang also offered a wider selection of V-8 engines than either of its competitors although the Camaro's optional 375-hp 396-cid V-8 had the edge on any other ponycar in straight-line performance.

In day-to-day driving, the Mustang was less roomy than the Barracuda and lacked the versatility of its large trunk, fold-down back seat, and removable trunk partition. The Mustang rode a bit harder than the Camaro, and was noisier than either the Camaro or Barracuda. On the other hand, it offered a neat option the others didn't: the Thunderbird-derived swing-away steering wheel. Also, Mustang convertible tops had a rear window made of articulated glass, which was superior to plastic. All three cars were well styled, and buyer preference was largely a matter of individual styling tastes.

Competition from the Big Three rivals—including its corporate cousin, Mercury Cougar—naturally hurt Mustang sales during 1967. Sales for the model year were down approximately 25 percent from 1966. Much of the loss was suffered by the best-selling hardtop. The convertible and fastback exchanged places in the sales race. The convertible dropped to only about 45,000 units, while the fastback moved up to over 70,000 by virtue of its slick new styling. But 472,121 sales was hardly a bad record for any car made by any company. In 1967, the Mustang success story continued as it had since the car's introduction.

Almost as if to answer the question of some Ford planners ("Why change a good thing?"), Mustang sales plummeted in 1968. On paper the losses were difficult to explain. It was a year of improving sales for the industry in general, including Ford Division. And

1968 Mustang convertible

The 1968 hardtop displayed only minor changes from '67.

This '68 GT fastback wears optional "C-stripes."

1968 Mustang GT fastback

Hood scoops and striping were new options for '68.

The GT/SC was a special model offered in mid-1968.

Taillights on GT/SC were similar to those on the GT-350.

Mustang offered the widest selection of engines and other options in its brief history.

The probable explanation is continued competition, which was rougher than ever in the now-crowded ponycar field. GM and Chrysler were out with new variations on the long hood-short deck theme. Even American Motors was a threat, with its new Javelin and AMX. Also, Mustang prices had risen since 1967. The 1968 convertible had a base list price of over $2,800, for example. A handful of options could run that to over $4,000—quite a sum in that year.

Significant, too, was competition from other Ford products. The Mustang fastback, which dropped in sales from over 70,000 to about 40,000 in 1968, had a major rival in the Ford Torino. This intermediate fastback, based on the '68 Fairlane, was the replacement for the 1967 Fairlane 500XL and GT muscle cars. It was visibly larger than the Mustang—201 inches in overall length compared to the Mustang's 184—and it had a genuine rear seat because its 116-inch wheelbase was eight inches longer than the Mustang's. The Torino's sleek fastback styling was quite similar to Mustang's, as were rival fastbacks like the Dodge Charger and Plymouth Barracuda. The Torino accounted for almost 54,000 sales in 1968, and it is reasonable to suggest that a healthy portion of those would have otherwise been Mustang fastbacks.

Since a fairly major face-lift had been carried out in 1967, the Mustang wasn't substantially altered for 1968. The three body styles—hardtop, convertible, and fastback—were continued. New rear quarter panels had the trademark simulated air scoops just ahead of the rear wheels, but these were integrated with the side sculpture for the first time. Crease lines ran back from the upper front fender around the fender scoop and forward again into the lower part of the door. On GT models, the sculpture was accented with tape striping, which gave the cars a look of forward motion.

The 1968 Mustang grille was deeply inset, with an inner bright ring around the familiar galloping horse. On GT models, fog lamps were contained within the grille opening. The GT equipment package remained essentially unchanged. In addition to side striping and fog lights, it included dual exhausts with chrome-plated "quad" outlets, a pop-open fuel filler cap, heavy-duty suspension (high-rate springs plus HD shocks and front sway bar), F70-14 whitewall tires on six-inch rims, and styled steel wheels. Wide-Oval tires could also be ordered.

The 1968 Mustang offered a vast array of engines, though some had been detuned to meet the new federal emission standards which went into effect that year. The compression ratio of the basic 200-cid six was lowered from 9.2:1 to 8.8:1, and output dropped slightly to 115 instead of 120 hp. The two-barrel 289 V-8 had a similar compression reduction, and was rated at 195 instead of 200 hp. The 390 engine was retained, but its horsepower increased to 335.

The middle-performance engine was a considerably changed version of the small-block, and was stroked out to 302 cubic inches (bore and stroke 4.00 x 3.00 inches), in which form it produced 230 hp. As before, it was a tractable, reasonably economical compromise between the basic V-8 and the High-Performance units. It added about $200 to the cost of a Mustang. The top of the engine lineup for 1968 (at a whopping $755 extra) was a mighty 427 cubic-inch V-8 with

10.9:1 compression and 390 hp.

Standard transmission on most '68 Mustangs was the three-speed manual all-synchromesh gearbox. The 271-hp V-8 continued with a choice of four-speed or Cruise-O-Matic, while the 427 came with Cruise-O-Matic only.

Safety features were big news in 1968. Some of those were added at Ford's discretion, but most were required by the government. These consisted of: energy-absorbing instrument panel and steering column, front and rear retractable seatbelts, back-up lights, dual-circuit brake system, hazard warning flashers, side marker lights, energy-absorbing seat backs, self-locking folding seats, positive door lock buttons, safety door handles, double-yoke door latches, padded sun visors and windshield pillars, double-thick laminated windshield, day/night rearview mirror on breakaway mount, outside rearview mirror, safety-rim wheels, and load-rated tires. The specifications also included corrosion-resistant brake lines and a standardized shift quadrant for the automatic transmission. To meet government standards for glare reduction, Ford put a dull finish on windshield wiper arms, steering wheel hub and horn ring, rearview mirror, and windshield pillars. Features that had been introduced the year before were reversible keys and 6,000-mile lube and oil change intervals. Another popular Ford feature was the 5/50-24/24 warranty. The powertrain, suspension, steering, and wheels were warranted for five years or 50,000 miles, whichever came first; other components were warranted for 24 months or 24,000 miles. The second retail purchaser could transfer the unused portion of the guarantee for a fee not exceeding $25.

The 427 Mustang was, at its price, intended only for very serious drivers. The 427 was an enormous engine for a car as light as the Mustang, and had one major disadvantage: It could be ordered only with the automatic. While 427 Mustangs were capable of 0-to-60 times of around only six or seven seconds, they oversteered heavily, a handling trait more familiar to racing drivers than to the average motorist. For the average driver, the 390 remained a much more flexible and practical engine. It could be had with four-speed or three-speed manual transmission as well as automatic, and it could produce over 15 miles per gallon if driven conservatively. It was a tractable engine in traffic, it idled smoothly, and was mild mannered at low speeds. Although it added some extra weight to the front end compared with smaller Mustang engines, this wasn't noticeable to the everyday driver unless he poked his foot to the floor.

The 390-engined cars benefitted in 1968 by the addition of floating-caliper power front disc brakes optional at extra cost. These brakes provided more stopping force with the same amount of pedal pressure as the '67 Mustang's brakes required. The floating caliper design was also said to promote longer brake life because it used fewer parts than previous Mustang disc brakes. Ford recognized the need for front discs in big-engined Mustangs by making them a mandatory

Specifications

Model Year Production

No.	Model	1966	1967	1968
63A	Fastback, standard	27,809	53,651	33,585
63B	Fastback, deluxe	7,889	17,391	7,661
63C	Fastback, bench seats	—	—	1,079
63D	Fastback, del. bench seats	—	—	256
65A	Hardtop, standard	422,416	325,853	233,472
65B	Hardtop, deluxe	55,938	22,228	9,009
65C	Hardtop, bench seats	21,397	8,190	6,113
65D	Hardtop, del. bench seats	—	—	853
76A	Convertible, standard	56,409	38,751	22,037
76B	Convertible, deluxe	12,520	4,848	3,339
76C	Convertible, bench seats	3,190	1,209	—
	TOTAL	607,568	472,121	317,404

Prices/Weights

Models	1966	1967	1968
01 hardtop, 6	$2,416/2,488	$2,461/2,568	$2,602/2,635
03 convertible, 6	$2,653/2,650	$2,698/2,738	$2,814/2,745
02 fastback, 6	$2,607/2,519	$2,592/2,605	$2,712/2,659

General Specifications	1966	1967	1968
Wheelbase:	108.0	108.0	108.0
Overall length:	181.6	183.6	183.6
Overall width:	68.2	70.9	70.9
Std. Trans.:	3-speed manual	3-speed manual	3-speed manual
Optional Trans:	4-speed manual 3-speed automatic	4-speed manual 3-speed automatic	4-speed manual 3-speed automatic

Engine Availability

Type	CID	HP	1966	1967	1968
I-6	200	120	Std.	Std.	—
I-6	200	115	—	—	Std.
V-8	289	195/200	Opt.	Opt.	Opt.
V-8	289	225	Opt.	Opt.	—
V-8	289	271	Opt.	Opt.	Opt.
V-8	302	230	—	—	Opt.
V-8	390	320/335	—	Opt.	Opt.
V-8	427	390	—	—	Opt.

option for all cars equipped with a 390 or 427 powerplant.

At over 300,000 units for 1968, Mustang sales were hardly great. And this figure was far below the heady period of 1965-66 when Iacocca's brainchild had earned over one million sales. For 1969, then, Ford decided on several new approaches to reverse the declining sales trend. The basic body package and 108-inch wheelbase were retained but the Mustang was redesigned to be more competitive in both the luxury and performance segments of the ponycar market. The result was the 1969 Grande and Mach I.

Shelby's Magic: GT-350 and GT-500

The year 1965 doesn't seem that long ago. Yet, 15-year-olds are hearing tales of how it was "in the good old days" when cars were vastly different, gas was dirt cheap, and the name of the game was "Total Performance."

Today it may be hard to realize that in 1965 a Shelby GT-350 could be driven right off the showroom floor. Even though this exotic Mustang variation was sold by selected Ford dealers, the GT-350 had all the trappings of speed and power: mag wheels, tachometer, glass-packed mufflers with side-exit pipes, a fiberglass hood, a trunk-mounted battery, and an engine which

had a higher number for horsepower than for cubic inches. And there was more: steel-tube exhaust headers, aluminum high-rise intake manifold, four-speed close-ratio transmission, Koni shocks, Detroit "Locker" rear end—all stock. Today's youngsters may just not believe it. But then, many people didn't believe it even in 1965. Carroll Shelby was different. When it came to cars, nobody ever convinced Ol' Shel that it couldn't be done.

To some, the name Carroll Shelby evokes memories of a disarming country boy with a wide "aw shucks" grin under a black cowboy hat. To more knowledge-

1964 Cobra 260

1965 Shelby GT-350

1965 Shelby GT-350 poses near Shelby plant at Los Angeles International Airport.

able auto enthusiasts, he was the man who built the Cobra, probably the fastest and hairiest sports car of all time. Shelby's rags-to-riches, back-to-rags, back-to-riches story is the stuff of which movies are made. At various times a truck driver, roustabout, ranch hand, salesman, and chicken farmer, Shelby began racing sports cars comparatively late in life. In the mid-1950's Shelby first drove MGs, then progressed to Ferraris, Maseratis, and Aston Martins. He was a good driver—maybe even sensational. But sports car racing was a gentleman's sport in those days. There was no prize money worth talking about. A driver like Shelby who wasn't independently wealthy had to have a sponsor who would supply the car and pay the expenses of racing it. Carroll Shelby had no problem promoting himself or his driving ability, and he delivered on those promises time and time again. By the time he won the prestigious 24 Hours of Le Mans in 1959, Shelby was riding a bubble on top of the world. That bubble burst when heart trouble forced him into retirement in the early '60s.

Shelby settled in southern California and made cars his business. First, he bought a Goodyear tire distributorship. Then, he started the first high-performance driving school in the U.S. He also nurtured a private dream: He would build a car of his own someday—the world's fastest production sports car. But without capital, and no firm design ideas, Shelby's vision remained only that. Then, fate took a hand. Shelby had heard that Ford was developing a small lightweight V-8 engine, the famous Fairlane 221—later enlarged to 260 and eventually to 289 cubic inches. At about the same time, it appeared AC Cars Ltd. of Surrey, England, was about to go out of business since the firm suddenly lost its supplier of engines for its strong, lightweight open sports car, the Ace. Shelby stepped in at precisely the right moment, dropped the Ford engine into the AC sports car, and the Cobra was born.

The Cobra soon became a household word—at least in the households of car enthusiasts. In their minds, the Shelby name became inextricably linked to Ford's performance image in the early and middle '60s, and "Cobra" became synonymous with horsepower. The reason: Cobras were winning almost every race in sight, including the coveted World Manufacturer's Championship for GT cars, a title which was held by Ferrari for 12 years before it was grudgingly yielded to Shelby.

The Cobra "rub-off" onto Ford's regular product line was of enormous value to Dearborn. Ford had already discovered the youth market and had launched the Mustang to capture it. Though initial Mustang sales had been higher than anyone at Ford expected, the car lacked a distinct high-performance image. So, Ford asked Shelby to race Mustangs against the Corvettes in Sports Car Club of America (SCCA) competition—and to win. Flushed with the Cobra's success, and knowing his way around race tracks and the sanctioning bodies, Shelby had a predictable reply: "Build a hundred of 'em." That was the minimum number which had to be built in order for a car to be qualified (or

"homologated") as a production-class racer.

As a first step, Shelby built two prototypes that started out as two ordinary Mustang fastbacks. A team of engineers and development drivers made numerous changes which transformed the soft, boulevard "sporty cars" into muscular racers that still looked a lot like the production Mustang. After all, if Ford was going to get any publicity benefit from its racing effort, the cars would still need to be recognizeable as Mustangs. Another goal of the Shelby program was to develop a Ford alternative to the Corvette. (The Cobra, although sold through selected Ford dealers, had always been regarded as an AC or a Shelby, not a Ford.)

Once the final specifications for Shelby's redesigned Mustang had been determined, a dozen white fastbacks were built at the Cobra production facility in Venice, California in late 1964. Another 100 white fastbacks ready for conversion were soon shipped to Venice from Ford's San Jose, California assembly plant. When SCCA inspectors arrived at the Shelby workshops to approve the model for production racing, they were somewhat surprised to find that more than the required minimum of 100 cars had been completed.

Just what did Shelby do to create these very special Mustangs? The formula was never a secret. These cars were certainly different from their mass-production brothers, but they still looked like Mustangs and that was important. It was this similarity in appearance that allowed the excitement of the Shelby Mustangs to rub off onto the more ordinary models. As a result, Ford's ponycar got exactly the kind of performance image the company wanted.

The Shelby formula was to start with a Mustang specially built to be modified by the Shelby factory and supplied with as many Ford parts as possible (although not necessarily Mustang parts). Each car to be converted was delivered by Ford as a white fastback with a black interior, 271-hp High-Performance engine, four-speed all-synchromesh manual transmission, Ford Galaxie rear end, and a long list of "delete items." Shelby-bound Mustangs were produced without hoods, exhaust systems, or rear seats. On the Shelby assembly line, each car received extensive suspension modifications, Koni shock absorbers, aluminum high-rise intake manifolds, finned aluminum valve covers and oil pan, special Holley carburetor, large front anti-sway bar, and a fiberglass hood with a functioning air scoop. Interior appointments included three-inch competition seat belts, a tachometer and oil pressure gauge mounted at eye level on the dashboard, and a wood-rimmed flat-dish racing-type steering wheel. Since there was no rear seat, the spare tire was relocated to the empty space for better weight distribution.

All 1965 Shelbys were white with black interiors—no other colors were used. They could also be identified (all Ford and Mustang emblems were removed), by their blue rocker-panel racing stripes which displayed the car's name—GT-350. Most of the early Shelby-Mustangs also had optional 10-inch-wide "Le Mans"

The GT-350 was often matched with the Jaguar XK-E (right) and Porsche 904 (rear) in SCCA B-Production races.

stripes, which ran from front to rear over the top of the car and were also blue. (American international racing colors are blue and white.)

Shelby's Mustang was originally conceived as a racing car, but most of the ones that were built saw duty on the street. Because Shelby realized that he could not easily sell 100 bona fide racing cars, he offered a standard model nearly identical in appearance with the racing version.

The most important feature of the R-model racer was the engine. SCCA rules specified that to qualify for production racing, a car's suspension or engine could be modified, but not both. Shelby chose to keep the same suspension components for both the street and competition versions of the GT-350 so that, under the rules, he could modify the engine. The street engine was based on Ford's 271-hp Hi-Performance 289, but used a hot cam, a large carburetor, and a less restrictive exhaust. It yielded an honest 306 hp. But the racing car engine also had special heads, and was rated at between 340 and 360 hp. The racing cars also weighed only 2,500 pounds, compared to 2,800 pounds for the street machines.

The GT-350 was homologated for SCCA "B-Production," which meant it would compete against small-block Corvettes, Sunbeam Tigers, Jaguar E-types, and the occasional Ferrari or Aston Martin. A total of 562 Shelby-Mustangs were built as 1965 models but no more than 30 of these were built to racing specifications. However, since all the special parts were available to private customers over the counter (per Shelby philosophy), anyone could turn their street car into the racing model by removing and/or substituting parts. Many owners did just that.

The GT-350 quickly established itself as the car to beat in B-Production and captured the national class championship from 1965 through 1967. Because GT-350s were so successful, it was naturally assumed a lot of them were competing. In fact, there weren't. What spectators saw were the same cars winning time after time. And, since the street cars looked so much like the racers, everyone assumed that they were all alike under the skin. This was, of course, a real ego boost for owners of the street cars, not to mention Ford Division.

To sell his earlier Cobra sports car, Shelby had established a network of performance-oriented Ford dealers, and he used this tactic again to get GT-350s into customer hands quickly. Although touted as "not the cars for everybody," they sold as rapidly as they could be built. The demand quickly exceeded the production capacity of Shelby's plant, which was also still making the Cobra. By the spring of 1965, the newly named Shelby American Inc. had moved from its Venice facility to two huge hangars on the edge of the Los Angeles International Airport.

The first batch of GT-350 street machines were made available to members of the automotive press for road testing. Virtually every major publication reported on the car but because it had no obvious competitor, most journalists could do little more than describe the GT-350 and its sizzling performance. GT-350s were loud, rough-riding, and a real effort to drive. But the driver was rewarded by the car's instant response. Function was the key word. Anything that did not contribute to the car's purpose—to go fast, handle well, and stop quickly—was either modified or thrown out.

In 1965 the Shelby GT-350 sold for $4,547, which was about $1,000 more than a standard Mustang and an equal amount less than the Corvette. This pricing put it right in the middle of the performance market. With 0-to-60 times averaging 6.5 seconds, a top speed of 130 to 135 mph, and race car handling and braking, the car drew rave reviews. It soon became something of a legend, and began to influence Detroit. Suddenly, scoops and rocker panel stripes began appearing on all sorts of production cars. While other manufacturers never actually offered a car in the same league as the GT-350, quite a few thought they did.

At the time the 1966 Shelby-Mustang was being planned, a lot was also happening at Ford. The company's all-out exotic performance car, the Ford GT, was faltering in international competition, so responsibility for the GT racing program was handed over to Carroll Shelby. Ford wanted the GT to carry its banner to the winner's circle at race tracks around the world. Since the company had invested a lot of money and faith in Shelby American, it wanted to see a tangible return on its investment—a competitive Ford GT. Shelby had a lot more on his mind in 1966 than the GT-350 alone.

Feedback from dealers and customers influenced some of the design changes made to the 1966 GT-350. The '65 was a good car, but without a back seat it was too impractical for the buyer with a family. (The rear seat had been omitted not merely so the spare tire could be relocated but to qualify the GT-350 under SCCA rules.) Also, the noisy, lurching Detroit "Locker" rear end was unnerving to those not acquainted with it. It howled and clunked at low speeds. The side-exit exhaust system was *very* loud—and illegal in some states. And the policy of "any color you want, so long as it's white" did not appeal to some buyers. From Ford came a demand for something called "cost-effectiveness:" Can the cost of each item or modification be justified by sales? Meantime, the Shelby people were trying to explain roadability to the accountants.

In effect, the changes made to the 1966 GT-350 were brought about by buyers and potential buyers—not by Carroll Shelby. In concept and as a finished car, the 1966 model was not the sort of thing Ol' Shel would have built if the choice were left up to him alone. Shelby buyers seemed to want performance all right, but without sacrificing other automotive virtues. So, starting in 1966, the Shelby-Mustang began to evolve into a car with broader market appeal. And as more cars were sold each year, the Shelby became more like the standard Mustangs and less like the semi-race car it started out to be.

Most of the revisions on the 1966 model could have been carried out on Ford's assembly line. However, Shelby did not always incorporate specific changes with the first car of a new model year. Instead, parts on hand were used up before new parts were ordered. Thus, there is no clear distinction between 1965 and 1966 models—appropriate for a limited-production manufacturer like Shelby. The first 250 1966 models (approximately) were leftover 1965s. They received all the 1966 cosmetic touches—a new grille, side scoops, and rear quarter windows. But they retained the 1965 suspension, Koni shocks, and 1965-style interior, and all were still painted white.

When actual 1966 production began, color choices were expanded to red, blue, green, and black, all offered with white racing stripes. A fold-down rear seat, standard on Mustang fastbacks, became a Shelby option. Almost all the 1966 GT-350s had it for an obvious reason: It was easier, and more profitable, for Ford to leave it in during initial assembly than for Shelby to remove the seat and install a one-piece fiberglass rear shelf. Batteries were left in their stock under-hood location. Heavy-duty Ford-installed shock absorbers were still used, as were the special Pitman and idler arms that gave the 1965 its sharp steering. The 1965 and early 1966 Shelbys used rear traction bars which ran from the inside of the car to the top of the rear axle; later models used Traction Master underride bars. Early cars also had lowered front A-arms, which altered the steering geometry for improved cornering. This refinement was determined

Ford GT40

Ford GT40 Mk2

Ford GT40 Mk2

not to be "cost effective," so it was discontinued on later '66 cars.

Engines and drivelines remained the same. The Detroit "Locker" rear end was made optional, as was an automatic transmission. All '66s, like the '65s, used large disc brakes in the front and large drums with sintered metallic linings in the rear. Extra pedal pressure was required with these brakes but they just didn't fade. The early 15-inch mag wheels (actually aluminum centers with steel rims) were replaced by 14-inch rims. These were either chrome styled steel or cast aluminum alloy wheels, at the buyer's option. All '66s received plexiglass rear quarter windows in place of the Mustang fastback's stock louvers used on '65 Shelbys.

Increased production was planned for 1966, so that every Shelby dealer who wanted cars could get them. Shelby also sold the Hertz Company on the idea of buying about 1,000 special "GT-350H" cars, all of which were finished in black with gold stripes. Hertz rented them at major airports throughout 1966. A lot of them were returned from a weekend's rental with definite signs of having been used in competition. Not surprisingly, Hertz soon found the GT-350H program a mite unprofitable.

Shelby-Mustang production in the second year was 2,380, including 936 Hertz models and six specially-built convertibles which Shelby gave away as gifts at the end of the model year. No racing cars were constructed, though a few leftover '65s were registered as 1966s. Shelbys continued to race and win that year, although they were essentially the same cars that had run the year before.

While the 1966 GT-350 wasn't quite as loud or fierce as the previous version, Shelby nevertheless kept it interesting. As an option, he offered a Paxton centrifugal supercharger. (A special GT-350S was envisioned, but never actually released.) The Paxton-blown engine was advertised with a horsepower increase of "up to 46 percent."

For 1967, production Mustangs were larger, heavier, and more "styled." This meant the GT-350 would have to change also. To keep the car's weight down and its appearance distinctive, Shelby stylists created a fiberglass front end to complement the production Mustang's longer hood. They also put two high-beam headlamps in the center of the grille opening. (Some later cars have these lamps moved to the outer ends of the grille to comply with state motor vehicle requirements specifying a minimum distance between headlamps.) The 1967 Shelbys had a larger hood scoop and sculptured brake cooling scoops on the sides. Another set of scoops on the rear-quarter roof panels acted as interior air extractors. The rear end received a spoiler and a large bank of taillights. As a total design, the 1967 Shelby was stunning. It looked more like a racing car than many racers. There was still nothing else like it.

Because the '67 was heavier than its predecessors, and because customer feedback indicated a preference for a more manageable car, power steering and power brakes were mandatory options. The new interior received some special appointments not shared with the production Mustang: a distinctive racing steering wheel, additional gauges, and a genuine rollbar with inertia-reel shoulder harnesses.

In 1967, Ford offered a 390 cubic-inch V-8 for its standard Mustang as its top performance engine. In typical Shelby style, Carroll went one better with a 428 cubic-incher and a new model, the GT-500. It was a highly popular move. GT-500s outsold GT-350s by a two-to-one margin. The GT-350 still carried the 271-hp engine warmed to Shelby specifications, but now without the steel-tube exhaust headers.

What Shelby had created was a combination of performance and luxury, cars that no longer emphasized performance above everything else. Since car makers adopted more conservative horsepower ratings in 1967—mainly to keep the insurance companies happy—the GT-500 was rated at only 355 hp, although it certainly developed more than that. The GT-350 was still rated at 306 hp, which is odd because without the headers and straight-through mufflers the output was certainly lower than this. No attempt was made by the factory to race the 1967 models. Altogether, 3,225 of them were built and sold.

By 1968, Carroll Shelby was beginning to tire of the car business. He'd won the Manufacturers Championship and had overseen the Ford GT effort culminating with wins at Le Mans in 1966 and 1967. He had also seen many close friends lose their lives on the race track. Meanwhile, competition had grown and new racing technology made it impossible for all but a few specialists to grasp new principles and apply them successfully. Racing, Shelby decided, wasn't fun anymore: It was business. And building his own cars had lost much of its original attraction because Ford was now calling most of the shots.

At the end of the 1967 model run, Shelby production was moved from Los Angeles to Michigan. The A.O. Smith Company was contracted to carry out Shelby conversions on stock Mustangs and Ford handled all promotion and advertising. The '68 Shelby received a face-lift: a new hood and nose, sequential rear turn signals, and a built-in rollbar for the convertible. GT-350s used Ford's new 302-cid engine. Luxury options like automatic transmission, air conditioning, tilt-type steering wheel, tinted glass, and AM-FM stereo now outnumbered performance features. In mid-year, the 428-cid engine was replaced with the 428 "Cobra Jet" unit which had made a name for itself on drag strips. Cars with this engine were called GT-500KR ("King of the Road"), and replaced the GT-500. Again in 1968, the big-block Shelbys were more popular, outselling the GT-350s by two-to-one. Total 1968 production was 4,450 cars.

By 1969, the federal government had introduced the first engine emission and safety regulations. Meanwhile, insurance premiums in the region of $1,000 were being quoted for 25-year-old males who drove quick cars. The taste of buyers had changed, too—performance was becoming less important than luxury.

Styling of the 1968 Shelby GT-500 was meant to convey "Total Performance."

The racy-looking 1968 Shelby GT-500 fastback.

Note integral roll bar on GT-500 convertible.

The 1968 GT-500 KR looks racy from any angle.

Shelby said "KR" stood for "King of the Road" in 1968.

Shelby saw the handwriting on the wall. Ever the individualist, he began by building the car he himself wanted to drive. He didn't like decisions made by committees where accountants and lawyers usually overruled the engineers and test drivers. And the niche he had created for his cars in the Ford lineup was gradually being filled by production Mustangs like the luxury Grande and the high-performance Mach I and Boss 302.

Mustang changed in 1969, and once more the Shelby changed with it. Shelby's stylists made the heavier, longer, busier production car look considerably more rakish. They extended the hood, fitted a fiberglass front end with a large grille cavity, used fiberglass front fenders for reduced weight, clipped off the tail, and added a spoiler and sequential turn signals. The GT-350 received the new 351 "Windsor" engine while the 428 CJ engine continued for the GT-500. The "KR" designation was dropped. Convertibles were still available. As usual, GT-500s outsold GT-350s and the total number of 1969 cars built was 3,150. Fuel injection had been considered for these cars, but was never adopted. A moonroof and reclining seats were other ideas that never made it into production.

At the end of the '69 model year, Carroll Shelby

1969 Shelby GT-500 was built in Michigan, not at the Shelby factory.

1969 Shelby GT-500 had more scoops and stripes than ever.

Wide taillights of '69 featured sequential turn signals.

called it quits. Production and design had become more Ford's responsibility than his. Competition from other cars built by Ford Division and other auto makers was much keener. His cars weren't being raced much any more and the later models were no longer the kind of cars he'd envisioned in the beginning. Ford Division executive vice president Lee Iacocca agreed to terminate the Shelby program. Cars still in the production pipeline at the end of 1969 were given Boss 302 front spoilers, black hood panels, and new 1970 serial

numbers. A little over 600 were made. Just like that, it was over.

After 1970, each succeeding year seemed to bring a less inspiring crop of cars as performance was redefined by Detroit. But as compression ratios were lowered and 0-to-60 times increased, many began to see the cars of Carroll Shelby in a new light. They became collector's items and their value started to increase. Today, a Shelby is worth twice what it sold for new. And there's justice in that.

Specifications

	Shelby Production By Model Year		
Year	GT-350	GT-500	Total
1965	562	—	562
1966	2,380*	—	2,380
1967	1,175	2,050	3,225
1968	1,648	2,802**	4,450
1969	1,279	1,871	3,150
1970	315	286	601

* includes 936 GT-350H models
** includes 1246 GT-500KR models

	Shelby Retail Prices, 1965-69			
	GT-350		GT-500	
Year	fastback	conv.	fastback	conv.
1965	$4,547	—	—	—
1966	$4,428	—	—	—
1967	$3,995	—	$4,195	—
1968	$4,117	$4,238	$4,317	$4,438
1969	$4,434	$4,753	$4,709	$5,027

Driving Impressions:
1966 and 1967
Shelby GT-350

Carroll Shelby's Mustangs reached their high point at the end of 1966. By then, Ford's corporate decision makers had succeeded in taming Shelby's brutes considerably. The 1967 and later models reflected this more conservative attitude and were not the racing-oriented cars their predecessors had been. Factors other than undiluted power were given attention: Styling and comfort were made part of the Shelby package. Nevertheless, the later cars were still Shelby-Mustangs and as such had their own distinct personalities.

For the sake of comparison we chose one of the last of the early Shelby GT-350s, and one of the first 1967 models. Both cars were set up more or less the same way making any basic differences in character or design more obvious.

Our test GT-350 was the 118th built in that model year. The first 250 or so cars built in 1966 were actually leftover 1965s updated with 1966 grilles, functional side brake cooling scoops, and plexiglass rear quarter windows. They still had the 1965 factory suspension which included lowered front A–arms, override rear traction bars, one-inch front sway bar, Koni shock absorbers, and modified Pitman and idler arms. Our car also had the optional fold-down rear seat from the production Mustang, plus the optional 15x6-inch Shelby-Cragar aluminum-center steel-rim wheels. Fresh from an exterior, undercarriage, and engine refurbishing, it still had its original white exterior paint and black interior. The untouched engine, which had covered some 60,000 miles, was the standard 289 cubic-inch, 306-hp powerplant and was stock right

Two generations of Shelby's GT-350 caught at rest: 1966 (left) and 1967 (right).

Note flamboyant lines of '67 GT-350 (right); '66 styling (left) was closer to that year's production Mustang.

down to the original steel-tube ("Tri-Y") exhaust headers and Holley 715 cfm center-pivot-float carburetor.

Our car's Borg-Warner T-10 four-speed gearbox carried the standard close-ratio gears but a Hurst shifter had been added because the stock Ford linkage leaves something to be desired (and was often described as "a baseball bat in a rain barrel" by Shelby enthusiasts.) Since the Hurst shift was offered as a factory option, this modification did not detract from the test car's authenticity. However, the standard original rear end had been changed on our car to the optional Detroit Automotive "No-Spin" unit. Because the original-equipment Goodyear Blue Dot 7.75x15 tires are no longer available, this '66 wore Goodyear Polyglas GTs, which are similar in size and performance.

The 1967 Shelby was rust-free when purchased by its present owner, and needed little more than a paint job to freshen its appearance. The engine and driveline had received some attention, with an eye toward reliability, since the car had already covered 70,000 miles. After the clutch, brakes, ball joints, and other components which deteriorate with age had been replaced, the car was as good as new—maybe better. One modification made to our car was the Detroit Automotive "No-Spin" rear end (optional in 1967 also). Other changes were use of steel-tube exhaust headers and the optional Shelby 15x7-inch aluminum alloy wheels. Goodyear GT radial tires (GR60x15) were fitted and are a vast improvement over the original E70x15 Goodyear "Speedway 350" bias-plys.

Both cars reflect different styling philosophies. The '66 seems to be a Mustang with certain things left off. The '67 has things added on. Compared to the stock Mustang, the '66 Shelby has larger tires, fewer emblems, twin over-the-top stripes, and a lower stance. The '67 Shelby is somewhat different in appearance from the corresponding stock Mustang—in some ways flagrantly so. Its nose is sharper, its grille cavity larger (with twin high-beam lights centered in the middle), scoops abound, there's a slick rear spoiler, and a large bank of taillights fills the back panel. Obviously, this is no ordinary 1967 Mustang.

The interiors of the two Shelbys are also different mainly because the stock Mustang interiors were redesigned for 1967. The most noticeable feature in the '66 is the "Cobra" 9000-rpm tachometer mounted on the dash at eye level. There are large three-inch competition seat belts that are perfectly in keeping with the car's "all-business" nature. Everything in the cockpit is finished in black. By contrast, the '67 uses the stock Mustang's deluxe interior with plenty of chrome and brushed aluminum on the dash. A factory tach sits in the dash beside the speedometer and Stewart-Warner gauges for oil pressure and amps are mounted under the dash as replacements for the stock units displaced by the tach. A wood-rimmed, three-spoke steering wheel is used and has a nice feel. But the '67s most striking feature is its genuine rollbar which houses a pair of inertia reels for the shoulder harnesses—the first ever used by an American production car. The '67's interior is also all black, but "parchment" was also available.

When started, both cars explode to life, then settle down to healthy-sounding exhaust notes. The clatter from the solid-lifter engines is amplified by those cast aluminum valve covers. Both cars sound as though they want to get out on the road *fast*. The 1966 car had manual steering, which made it a real chore to steer at low speeds. The Detroit "Locker" rear end lurches when the transmission is engaged. Interestingly enough, most enthusiasts enjoy this feature today, but it was considered undesirable back in the '60s, so Ford made the "Locker" an option after 1965.

The early Shelbys were light cars compared to the stock Mustangs and they performed better than stock partly because of this. Throttle response is instantaneous in all gears and the engine spins easily right up to its 7000-rpm redline. A twitch of the wheel is all that's needed to alter direction. In fast curves, a stab at the gas tends to bring the rear end out and straightens the line. There's relatively little body lean. Both cars feel poised, beautifully balanced, and ready for any kind of road.

Braking behavior in the '66 is more like that of a racing car than a street machine. Early Shelbys had larger disc brakes up front and oversize drum brakes with metallic segmented linings in the rear. Early GT-350s, including our test car, also had sintered metallic front disc pads which had to be thoroughly warmed up before they worked properly. As expected, our car wouldn't stop very quickly until the pads were warmed, but once they were, the brakes were amazingly good, pulling the car down from very high speeds in a straight line without a trace of fade.

Getting into the '67 GT-350, we were immediately aware of a difference in feel. Its power assist reduces steering effort at the wheel but at the expense of road feel. Although we didn't weigh either car, the '67 Shelby gives the impression of being heavier than the '66 and by more than the 70 pounds shown in the data table which lists figures taken from tests published when the cars were new.

Although both cars respond quickly to throttle, steering, and brakes, the '66 is loud and we mean *loud*. It also rides like the thinly disguised Trans-Am racer it is. By contrast, the '67 is smoother, quieter, and more civilized.

No one is likely to be bored driving cars like this—not even jaded enthusiasts. Both these Shelbys handle, go, and stop in a way that few of today's production cars can match except, perhaps, the expensive Italian exotics. In a world where most cars are designed just for getting people from point A to point B, the Shelby-Mustangs recall an age when driving was something more than just transportation. Even back in the '60s these cars, with their no-compromise character, were never in the same league with their competition. They were designed to be in a class by themselves. Today, Shelby-Mustangs still are.

Specifications

	1966 GT-350	1967 GT-350
Price when new:	$4,428	$4,195
Engine type, cylinders:	ohv V-8	ohv-V-8
Bore x Stroke (in.):	4.00x2.87	4.00x2.87
Displacement (cu. in.):	289	289
Compression ratio:		
Horsepower @ rpm:	306 (gross) @ 6000	306 (gross) @ 6000
Transmission type/forward gears:	manual/4	manual/4
Final drive ratio:	3.89:1	3.89:1
Tire size:	7.75x15	E70x15
Steering, turns lock-to-lock:	3.75	4.0
Turning diameter (ft.):	38	37
Brake swept area (sq. in.):		
Curb weight (lbs.):	2850	2920
Weight distribution, front/rear	53/47	53/47
Wheelbase (in.):	108	108
Overall length (in.):	181.6	186.6
Overall width (in.):	68.2	70.9
Track, front/rear (in.):	57/57	58/58
Height (in.):	51.2	51.6
Ground clearance (in.):	5.5	6.5
Suspension, front:	Independent; upper and lower A-arms, coil springs; tube shocks	
Suspension, rear:	Live axle; semi-elliptic leaf springs; tube shocks	
Performance		
pounds/horsepower (gross):	9.31	9.54
acceleration, 0-60 mph (sec.)	6.7	7.1
estimated top speed (mph)	132	129

Style and Stamina: 1969~70

The 1969 Mustang arrived shortly after Semon E. "Bunkie" Knudsen became president of Ford in early 1968. Under Knudsen, Ford vigorously emphasized racy styling and high performance. The Mustang reflected this by offering a new breed of grand touring and luxury models like the Mach I, Grande, and Boss 302.

While the 1969 Mustang retained the 108-inch wheelbase of the original '65-'68 cars, almost every other dimension was changed. The '69 was generally more roadable than its predecessors and some versions were also very quick. The Cobra Jet Mach I and Boss 302 were the quickest production Mustangs other than the Shelby GTs and were Ford's response to the challenge of the Camaro Z/28 and Firebird Trans Am.

When Bunkie Knudsen left General Motors as

1969 Mustang (base hardtop)

New-for-1969 Mustang Grande

executive vice-president to become president of Ford, Detroit gasped in astonishment. There probably hadn't been such a startling shift since Bunkie's father, William S. ("Big Bill") Knudsen left Ford after an argument with the elder Henry and went to Chevrolet. In the 1920's, "Big Bill" built Chevrolet into a Ford beater, and now his son was trying to make Ford more competitive with Chevrolet for the '70s.

Rumors about a drastic shakeup in Ford management began flying around Detroit almost as soon as Knudsen arrived in Dearborn for his first day on the job. Although some staff changes were expected, Knudsen didn't instigate a wholesale cleanout, and he certainly had Ford looking a lot more competitive within a few months of his arrival.

Knudsen's presidency meant a renaissance for the performance Mustang. What he wanted were lower, sleeker cars, with particular emphasis on the fastback. In fact, Knudsen said that while "the long-hood, short-deck concept will continue . . . there will be a trend toward designing cars for specific segments of the market." While Knudsen denied Ford had any intention of building a sports car, he did hint that an experimental mid-engine car was being developed. He also assured the press that Ford's efforts in stock car racing would continue. Knudsen was sanguine about the Mustang's market prospects, and the car's declining sales since 1966 didn't bother him. "We are comparing today's Mustang penetration with the penetration of the Mustang when there was no one else in that particular segment of the market. Today (it is) much more competitive."

One of Knudsen's more productive raids on his former employer resulted in the hiring of GM stylist Larry Shinoda to head Ford's Special Design Center. Shinoda was assisted by a talented crew which included Harvey Winn, Ken Dowd, Bill Shannon, and Dick Petit. Together with engineers like Chuck Mountain and Ed Hall, Shinoda's department conceived such eye-opening cars as the King Cobra, a racing Torino fastback. Shinoda's arrival at Ford was also good for the Mustang. Since the early '60s he had designed wind-cheating shapes like the original Sting Ray, Corvette Mako Shark, Monza GT, and Corvair Super Spyder for GM's William L. Mitchell. Shinoda favored the use of aerodynamic aids like spoilers, low noses, air foils, and front air dams. Many of these features would later appear on Mustangs and other Ford models.

Styling for the 1969 model was mostly completed by the time Shinoda arrived, and the dimensions of the new design marked a departure from the original Mustang. While it retained the previous car's wheelbase and long-hood, short-deck shape, the '69 Mustang was four inches longer, most of it in front overhang. It was also slightly wider and lower. The 1969 grille was similar to that of its predecessors, but two extra headlights were added at the outer ends in place of the optional but mostly ineffective fog lights. The recessed side sculpture of 1968 was erased. Taillights were still vertical clusters, but they were no longer recessed in the tail panel which was now flat instead of concave. The car's driving range was increased by enlarging the fuel tank from 17 to 20 gallons.

Dimensional increases were evident on the inside too. The 1969 model had 2.5 inches more front shoulder room and 1.5 inches more hiproom than previous versions because engineers had cut down on door thickness. A modified frame cross-member under the front seat allowed rear seat legroom to be increased by a significant 2.5 inches. Trunk capacity was enlarged "13 to 29 percent" according to bubbly Ford press releases, but actually this wasn't much of a gain because there wasn't much space to begin with. A Mustang trunk could just manage a two-suiter and not much else. As before, there were three basic body configurations—hardtop, fastback, and convertible—but there were several new permutations. Two appeared at the beginning of the model year, and the third in mid-season.

Taking careful aim at the personal-luxury market dominated by Cougar and Firebird, Ford Division released the six- and eight-cylinder Mustang Grande hardtop. Priced at about $230 over the standard hardtop, the Grande offered a vinyl-covered roof with identifying script; twin color-keyed outside rearview

Mach I was a new model for 1969. Note side scoop to the rear of the door.

The 1969 Mustang convertible, like the other models, was longer, lower, and wider than the year before.

mirrors; wire wheel covers; bright wheel well, rocker panel, and rear deck moldings; and a two-tone paint stripe just below the beltline. The Grande interior was decorated with imitation teakwood trim (a very good copy of the real thing) and the body used some 55 extra pounds of sound insulation.

A more lively Mustang variation was the Mach I, offered only with a V-8 engine at a $3,139 base price. As an intruder into Shelby territory, Mach I featured

1969 Mach I had hood pins and "Shaker" hood scoop.

1969 Mach I featured luxurious interior.

1970 Mustang Mach I Cobra Jet

simulated rear-quarter air scoops, a rear spoiler, and a functional hood scoop, nicknamed "The Shaker" by Ford engineers. The scoop was attached to the engine air cleaner, and stuck up through a hole in the hood. The scoop earned its name by vibrating madly, especially at high revs.

Though its dimensional differences from other Mustangs were slight, the Mach I was definitely the raciest looking model offered in 1969. Its broad, flat hood and sweeping roofline combined with NASCAR hood tie-downs and that aggressive hood scoop to create the aura of a genuine performance car. With a 351-cid engine and 250 hp in standard form, the Mach I didn't disappoint.

Engine options proliferated in 1969, extending even to the six-cylinder cars. For $39, a customer could order a larger 250-cid six with 155 hp. Ford greatly improved six-cylinder smoothness that year with "center percussion" (forward located) engine mounts. Competition manager Jacque Passino was optimistic about the six: "We've been putting out Mustang sixes kind of artificially since '64 to fill up production schedules when we couldn't get V-8s. I think there is a real market for an inexpensive hop-up kit for the 250 cubic-inch engine." But Passino was whistling in the wind. A hop-up kit never materialized, nor did a six-cylinder fuel-injected engine which he also predicted. Engineers never developed a performance version of the Mustang six, though they probably should have.

Mustang V-8 offerings began with the 302-cid engine of 220 hp, and ran to the top-line Cobra Jet 428 available with or without ram-air injection. The Mach I's 351-cid engine was available in other Mustangs and indeed in most other Ford products except the Falcon. Though derived from the 289/302, the 351 was really a new engine. Its deck height was greater and its combustion chamber design was different from the earlier small-blocks. It was also heavier than the 302, but much lighter than the big-block V-8s. For all-out performance the Cobra Jet was still king and with it, the Mach I was one of the world's fastest cars.

The Cobra Jet had been developed by Ford's Light Vehicle Powertrain Department under Tom Feaheney. For the Mach I it was thoughtfully combined with a tuned suspension designed by engineer Matt Donner. Donner used the 1967 heavy-duty suspension set-up, but mounted one rear shock ahead of the rear axle line and the other behind it to eliminate wheel hop. Result: A production Mustang that handled like a Trans-Am racer. The big-engine Mach I still exhibited final oversteer, but the rear end was easily controllable with the accelerator pedal.

"The first Cobra Jets we built were strictly for drag racing," Feaheney said. "The '69s had a type of the competition suspension we offered in '67. Wheel hop was damped out by staggering the rear shocks. It was not a new idea but it worked. Another thing was the (Goodyear) Polyglas tire. I really can't say enough about this. . . In '69 every wide-oval tire we offered featured Polyglas construction." All this talk of handling may obscure the matter of straight-line performance. Just for the record, the Cobra Jet Mach I would run the quarter-mile in about 13.5 seconds. And that was as good as any production four-seater in 1969.

With styling help from Larry Shinoda, Ford released an even more exotic Mustang in early 1969, the Boss 302. This car was primarily created to compete with the Camaro Z/28, in SCCA's Trans-Am series. (See chapter 13). To qualify it as a production racer, Ford had to build at least 1,000 copies; actually 1,934 were constructed in 1969. But inspite of its low production, the Boss brought people into Ford showrooms like the original Mustang did back in 1964. Knudsen knew what grabbed the public.

Among Shinoda's design touches were the addition of front and rear spoilers which were effective at any speed over 40 mph. The four-inch-wide front spoiler was angled forward to divert air away from underneath the car. The rear spoiler was an adjustable, inverted airfoil. Matte black rear window slats, like those of the Lamborghini Miura, did nothing to enhance airflow but looked terrific. The aerodynamic aids resulted in a gain of perhaps 2.5 seconds per lap at Riverside with no increase in engine power. Of course, there *was* an increase in engine power—a big one.

The Boss 302 engine was said to produce 290 hp at 4600 rpm, but estimates of its actual horsepower ranged as high as 400 hp. The engine used "Cleve-

land" heads with oversize intake valves and huge 1.75-inch exhaust valves which were inclined in the enormous ports to improve fuel flow. Other engine features consisted of an aluminum high-rise manifold, Holley four-barrel carburetor, dual-point ignition, solid lifters, bolted central main bearings, forged crankshaft, and special pistons.

The Boss 302 came with ultra-stiff spring rates, staggered shocks, a Stout CJ four-speed gearbox, 11.3-inch power front disc brakes, heavy-duty rear drum brakes, and F60x15 Goodyear Polyglas tires. To help prolong the life of the potent engine, Ford fitted an ignition cut-out which interrupted current flow from the coil to the spark plugs between 5800 and 6000 rpm, encouraging the driver to shift. Ford hadn't missed a trick: Even the wheel wells were radiused to accept extra-wide racing tires. On the street, Boss 302s were unmistakable in appearance. They had a matte black center hood section and grille extensions plus special striping with "Boss 302" lettering. In 1969 they were the ultimate Mustangs.

Mustang's expansion into the upper ends of both the luxury and performance fields produced some interesting results. Out of 184,000 cars delivered in the first half of 1969, only about 15,000 were Grandes but close to 46,000 were Mach Is. On cue, Division general manager John Naughton predicted "heavy emphasis on performance" for what he—or his press writers—

The 1970 Boss 302 was Ford's factory-built Mustang racer.

1970 Mustang Boss 302

Mustang Mach I for 1970

1970 Mustang (base fastback)

1970 Mustang fastback with Boss-type C-stripes

1970 Mustang Grande prototype

1970 Mustang Grande

saw as the "Sizzlin '70s." Said Naughton: "We're going to be where the action is, and we're going to have the hardware to meet the action requirements of buyers everywhere." The Mach I, Naughton continued, would be Ford's big gun in the performance race. The Boss 302 and the even hairier 1970 Boss 429 were intended for the outer fringes of the market—and the Trans-Am. Two Boss styling features, backlight louvers and adjustable rear spoiler, had such an impact they were offered for any Mustang "SportsRoof" (fastback). Ford, said Naughton, was going to "make it happen in 1970."

And in a way, Ford did. The 1970 Boss, as *Motor Trend* put it, was "even Bossier" than it had been the year before. Unique side paint striping identified it; a well-engineered suspension cornered it; and hotter-than-ever engines powered it. New for 1970 was a Hurst competition shifter with T-handle shift knob, the first Hurst linkage offered by Ford in a production Mustang. Further up the price scale at around $4,000 was the promised Boss 429, which used Ford's Cobra Jet NASCAR engine. This engine was even more potent than the other big-inch V-8s. It had cast magnesium rocker arm covers and semi-hemispherical combustion chambers. Valves were set across from each other for a crossflow cylinder head and the ports, intake passages, and oval exhausts were all enormous.

Mach I engines for 1970 ranged from the 351-cid two-barrel V-8 up to the 428 four-barrel with ram air. The Cleveland engine was further improved over the 1969 version by canted-valve cylinder heads, larger intake and exhaust ports, and a block and rods designed for extra durability like the 429 racing engine. Mach I suspension was also improved with the addition of a rear stabilizer bar which helped the car corner flat and level, yet allowed the use of moderate spring rates for a decent ride. The 1970 Mach I featured its own special grille with driving lamps. Carried over from 1969 were the dull-finish black center hood section, hood locks, the functional hood scoop, twin racing mirrors, pop-open gas cap, and black honeycomb rear panel applique.

The Grande was still offered with either six or V-8 engines. Like all Mustangs for 1970, it inherited the high-back front bucket seats of the Mach I which added greatly to interior comfort. A landau-style black or white vinyl roof, twin racing-type mirrors, special identification, and bright wheel lip moldings completed the package.

There were still "basic" Mustangs in 1970 available with standard six or 302 V-8 engines in hardtop, convertible, and SportsRoof fastback body styles. Like other models, they boasted new front-end styling and reverted to single headlights. Rear-end styling was revised with recessed taillamps. Prices still hadn't climbed much since the Mustang's early days. A six-cylinder coupe listed at only a bit more than $2,700, and a V-8 convertible could be had for as little as $3,126. Convertibles, though, were on the wane: Production dipped to only about 7,700 in 1970. Continuing buyer preference for air conditioning and closed coupes had conspired to reduce the popularity of convertibles in general and made the Mustang ragtop relatively rare.

Despite an exciting lineup of models, Mustang production dropped by another 100,000 units in 1970. Fastbacks slipped 40 percent while hardtops were down 35 percent. Convertibles were almost non-existent. While the Mach I accounted for a solid proportion of fastback sales, it was not a high volume seller. It couldn't make up for continuing strong opposition by other performance models from Ford and rival manufacturers. The Boss 302 remained strictly as a limited-production Trans-Am special with low sales potential: Output was just 6,318 units for 1970. Ford Division was going to have to take a long, hard look at its ponycar for 1971.

One reason changes were made to the '71 Mustang had to do with top management. After just two years as president, Bunkie Knudsen was summarily dismissed. Said chairman Henry Ford II: "Things just didn't work out." Ford never elaborated on that statement. Ford's longtime motto is "never complain, never explain." Insiders suggested that, like his father before him, Knudsen had accumulated—and was wielding—too much power. "Knudsen moved in and started doing things his way," writes prominent Detroit analyst Robert W. Irvin. "Knudsen was almost running the company and (some said) he had alienated many other top executives. Others said Knudsen's departure was an indication of how the Fords don't like to share power." Irvin wrote those words in July, 1978, as a comment on the firing of Lee A. Iacocca. There's a long history of top-rung shakeups at the Ford Motor Company.

In 1969, however, it looked as if Lee Iacocca could do no wrong. To soften the impact of Knudsen's dismissal, Henry Ford II announced there would be three Ford presidents: R. L. Stevenson for International Operations, R. J. Hampson for Non-Automotive Operations, and Iacocca for North American Operations. But that triumvirate lasted only a year: Iacocca became overall president in 1970. And dramatic changes were planned for the 1971 Mustang.

Of course, Iacocca didn't have much to do with these alterations, as Knudsen had already influenced the design of the '71s. But one cold hard fact was staring Mustang planners in the face and it was hard to ignore: Cars with the "Total Performance" image were no longer appealing to buyers, at least not in really high volume.

In late 1970, Ford abandoned most of its efforts in Trans-Am, USAC, NASCAR, and international competition. It also began to change the Mustang's character. After the cars called the "Sizzlin '70s," the 1971 Mustangs would seem tame.

Specifications

Model Year Production

No.	Model	1969	1970
63A	Fastback, standard	56,022	39,470
63B	Fastback, deluxe	5,958	6,464
63C	Fastback, Mach 1	72,458	40,970
65A	Hardtop, standard	118,613	77,161
65B	Hardtop, deluxe	5,210	5,408
65C	Hardtop, bench seats	4,131	—
65D	Hardtop, del. bench seats	504	—
65E	Hardtop, Grande	22,182	13,581
76A	Convertible, standard	11,307	6,199
76B	Convertible, deluxe	3,439	1,474
	TOTAL	299,824	190,727

Models	Prices/Weights	
	1969	1970
01 hardtop, 6	$2,635/2,690	$2,721/2,721
02 fastback, 6	$2,635/2,713	$2,771/2,745
03 convertible, 6	$2,849/2,800	$3,025/2,831
04 Grandé, 6	$2,866/2,765	$2,926/2,806
01 hardtop, V-8	$2,740/2,906	$2,822/2,923
02 fastback, V-8	$2,740/2,930	$2,872/2,947
02 Boss 302, V-8	$3,588/3,210	$3,720/3,227
03 convertible, V-8	$2,954/3,016	$3,126/3,033
04 Grandé, V-8	$2,971/2,981	$3,028/3,008
05 Mach 1, V-8	$3,139/3,175	$3,271/3,240

General Specifications	1969	1970
Wheelbase:	108.0	108.0
Overall length:	187.4	187.4
Overall width:	71.3	71.7
Std. Trans.:	3-speed manual	3-speed manual
Optional Trans.:	4-speed manual	4-speed manual
	3-speed automatic	3-speed automatic

Engine Availability

Type	CID	HP	1969	1970
I-6	200	115	Std.	Std.
I-6	250	155	Opt.	Opt.
V-8	302	220	Std.[a]	Std.
V-8	351	250	Opt.[b]	Opt.[b]
V-8	351	290/300	Opt.	Opt.
V-8	390	320	Opt.	—
V-8	428	335	Opt.	Opt.
V-8	428[c]	335	Opt.	Opt.

a 290 hp std. Boss 302
b Std. Mach I
c with Ram Air

Is This the Way We Want to Go: 1971-73

No Mustang history would be complete without mention of the intriguing mid-engine Mach 2. Exactly where this fascinating design exercise fits in the Mustang story is difficult to say. It began as early as 1966 and the car was still around in 1970. If nothing else, the existence of the Mach 2 indicated just how many ideas were being considered for future Mustang designs long after the basic concept had proven to be a sales winner. The Mach 2 is certainly part of the Mustang family; it would not have been built otherwise.

Despite Bunkie Knudsen's denials, Ford hadn't quite given up on a two-seater car when he arrived as president. The mid-engine GT-40 had been developed into one of the finest endurance racers of all time, as its world-wide competition success proved. Sales executives eyed exotic Ford-powered foreign cars, like the De Tomaso Mangusta, with envy. Once again there arose the question that led to every low-volume specialty Ford from the 1946 Sportsman to the two-seat Thunderbird: Why not build something to attract people to the showrooms—to promote the overall Ford product image?

The project to develop a mid-engine car had the same goal that had guided creation of the original Mustang: Use as many off-the-shelf components as possible, wrapped up in a revolutionary new package. Ford developmental engineer Ed Hull used a Mustang engine and German ZF five-speed transaxle. The original boxed side frame rails were connected by a cross-member at the point where they were humped to clear the now-discarded live rear axle, and the platform was cut aft of this point. The crossmember served to strengthen the shortened floorpan and acted as an engine support. A frame made of square steel tubes was added to the front of the chassis and provided attachment points for the body and front suspension. Though the original driveshaft tunnel would be otherwise unnecessary with the mid-engine layout, it was used as a housing for control pipes and water hoses. The radiator was left in its front-mounted position.

The Mach 2's rear suspension was inspired by Lotus. The transaxle half-shafts acted as upper suspension arms and there were lower links with parallel trailing arms to guide the hub carriers and absorb braking torque. Said Hull in an interview with writer Karl Ludvigsen: "It wasn't easy getting those arms past the frame rails and keeping good geometry. It took me a stack of computer print-outs *this* high." Coil springs enclosing adjustable Koni shocks completed the rear suspension.

The rest of the chassis was made up of absolutely stock Ford components: The front suspension, disc brakes, and quick-ratio manual steering came from the Mustang while Galaxie-size drum brakes were used at the rear. The body, made of fiberglass to save time and money, was attached to the platform with adhesives, which held it in place yet allowed for some flexing.

The Mach 2 must have opened a few eyes at Chevrolet, even though Ford's chief rival had dabbled

Ford's Mach 2 mid-engine prototype was based on shortened Mustang chassis.

This 1969 clay featured Torino-like styling.

A refined version was dubbed "Apex."

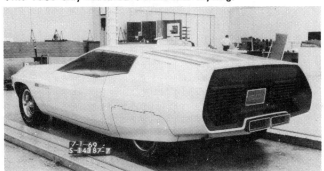
Ford considered this wild-looking design.

Like car on the left, this idea never made it.

Study called "302 Mustang" had clean front end.

This Maverick coupe might have replaced Mustang in '71.

with the mid-engine concept for some time. Chevy's Astro II show car was close in concept to the Mach 2, as was the Aerovette, which for a time was rumored to be a prototype for the next production Corvette. The Mach 2 was extensively tested for several years. It was followed by another study based on the Falcon/Maverick platform, and by other mid-engine prototypes. Ultimately, though, the Mach 2 was judged to have no potential for volume sales and so it remained just another dream car.

Even the conventional front-engine, rear-drive ponycar concept came in for evaluation by late 1969. At that time it was becoming increasingly clear that the ponycar was losing its appeal. Mustang sales had been sliding since 1968. Camaro and Firebird sales had held up, but were not improving. The AMC Javelin was a mild success, but no blockbuster. Neither were

the rebodied 1970 Plymouth Barracuda and its stablemate, the Dodge Challenger, which did not bring in the pile of orders Chrysler had expected. By 1971, compacts like the Pinto, Maverick, Vega, and Gremlin were cutting into ponycar sales which were down to almost half of what they had been in their best-ever year, 1967.

Given the auto industry's normal lead time, the shape of the '71 Mustang was really determined by the events of 1968-69. At that time, the effect new government regulations would have on future car design was still unknown and was still being debated. The idea that the world might soon run low on oil was not yet taken seriously by many people. So the product planners saw the ponycar's lack of sufficient interior space as the reason for the higher sales of the compacts. Ford's decision to make the next generation

Two-seater "Runabout" wasn't seriously considered.

Familiar themes were used on this mid-1970 study.

Another sleek fastback had lighter appearance.

This idea was also an early proposal for 1974.

By now, the 1971 design was locked up.

One of many ideas for post-1971 styling.

This muscular mock-up was considered when performance Mustangs were still hot sellers.

of Mustang larger, roomier, and heavier was perfectly logical in the context of the late '60s.

Buyer demand for more room and luxury determined much of the '71 design, but the influence of Ford's racing heritage was still evident. Of course, in 1969 nobody could have predicted that Ford would get out of racing only six months after the '71s appeared. That's why the sweeping, almost-horizontal roofline of Ford's GT racers eventually showed up on the 1971 Mustang "SportsRoof." The full-width grille scoops and rear deck scoops of the Shelby GTs were also picked up by Ford's designers. Available for 1971 were color-coordinated polyurethane front bumpers which helped the stylists shape a more interesting and better integrated front end. Larry Shinoda accompanied Bunkie Knudsen in departing from Ford in 1969 but not before he had styled the 1971 Mustang along the lines of the Shelby cars. Shinoda's GM background showed in the new car's body surface shaping, more acute windshield angle, and the use of hidden wipers as well as the "cockpit" interior.

The result of all this was the most changed Mustang since the original—fully restyled and as big as a Mustang would ever get. Though its wheelbase was only one inch longer than before, the '71 model was eight inches longer overall, six inches wider, and close to 600 pounds heavier than the '65 original. Though the familiar long-hood, short-deck proportions were retained for the longer body, the 1971 model was a more heavily "styled" car than the original Mustang.

Because more stringent emissions standards took effect in 1971, the number of Mustang engine offerings was reduced. The Boss 302 powerplant was replaced by the Boss 351 "Cleveland" engine with four-barrel carburetor, 11:1 compression ratio, and 330 hp (gross) at 5400 rpm. The Boss 351 was more tractable than the Boss 302, and, since it wasn't as high-revving, more durable. On other Mustangs, the standard V-8 was a 302 with two-barrel carb and 9:1 compression for 220 hp at 4600 rpm. The standard six was now the 250-cid unit with 8:1 compression and 145 hp at 4000 rpm. There were only two other optional V-8s—the ordinary four-barrel 302 with 285 gross horsepower, and the four-barrel 429-cid Cobra Jet with 370 hp.

The Mach 1 equipped with 429CJ engine could be ordered with air conditioning ($407) and automatic transmission ($238). In fact, the car could be outfitted with a whole host of convenience features: power steering, tilt steering wheel, "sport deck" rear seat, AM/FM stereo, and intermittent wipers. Special options included a sports interior ($130), power front disc brakes ($70), center console ($60), and an instrument group ($54). Liberal use of the option book could raise the price of a Mach I from its $3,268 base to $5,500. Standard Mach 1 equipment this year included high-back bucket seats, integrated front spoiler, honeycomb grille, dual exhausts, auxiliary lamps, and racing-style exterior mirrors. The 429CJ engine cost $436 extra.

The Mach I 429CJ was undeniably quick. It would do 0-to-60 mph in 6.5 seconds, 0-to-75 in about 9.0 seconds, and the quarter-mile in 14.5 seconds. With

1971 Boss 351

1971 Mach I

1971 Mustang convertible

1971 Mustang Grande

automatic transmission and 3.25:1 final drive ratio it had a top speed of about 115 mph and returned 10-11 miles per gallon. "It is a decent mixture for those who want good performance and some comfort," wrote Chuck Koch in *Motor Trend,* "but it still remains a little unwieldy for city traffic."

The Boss 351 tested by Koch handled better than the Mach I because it had the "competition" suspension as standard equipment. This consisted of independent coil springs and hydraulic shocks up front, staggered rear shocks, and front and rear stabilizer bars. With Koch at the wheel, the Boss 351 was even quicker than the Mach I 429. It did 0-to-60 in 10 seconds and the quarter-mile in 13.8 seconds. But, with the short rear axle ratio of 4.91:1, the Boss 351 would only reach about 100 mph flat out.

The 302 V-8 with 220 hp was no match for these very powerful Mustangs. Its figures were 0-to-60 in 10 seconds, the quarter-mile in 17.5 seconds, and a top speed (with 2.79:1 axle ratio and automatic) of only 86 mph. This was hardly sluggish, and the 302 delivered decent gas mileage in the Mustang of up to 17 mpg. All things considered, the 302 was probably the best all-around powerplant offered in '71.

With the perspective of hindsight the 1971 Mustang doesn't seem like a bad car even though it got a lot of "bad press" when it first appeared. It was made larger because buyers didn't like cars with cramped interiors. It was the thirstiest Mustang yet because with gas still selling for only 30 cents a gallon in those days, most buyers weren't too concerned about fuel economy. Yet, the '71 version, especially those with the competition suspension, rode and handled better than previous Mustangs. Understeer was greatly reduced, and roadholding was improved. Optional variable-ratio power steering gave it better road feel than in the past, despite the gains in weight and size. The low, flat-roof fastback design was racy looking and attractive in an era of somewhat uninspired styling.

But offering a good car does not necessarily mean

Mustang was mostly unchanged for '72 but Sprint decor option shown here was new.

1972 Mustang hardtop

1972 Mustang convertible

sales success, as Ford Motor Company knew all too well. If Mustang was not losing any customers to the Camaro, Firebird, and Barracuda, it was definitely being outsold by Maverick, Valiant, Dart, and Nova. As a result, Mustang sales sagged once again. Model year production totaled less than 150,000 units. Hardtop sales dropped to 83,000, the convertible captured a bit more than 6,000, and the fastback sold 60,000.

There is nothing to do with a one-year-old design in Detroit except live with it, so the 1972 Mustangs were little changed. The same engine lineup was offered, except for the Boss 351, which vanished. To meet 1972's lower emission levels Ford detuned the standard six and eight, as well as the three optional 351 V-8s. All horsepower figures were now expressed as SAE net, rather than gross, ratings. The 250-cid six was thus rated at 98 hp net at 4000 rpm and the 302 V-8 produced 110 hp net at 4600 rpm. The 351-cid engines produced from 162 to 223 hp. Again in 1972,

sales dipped, this time by about 20 percent. Only the convertible—which by now didn't account for many sales—maintained its previous level of around 6,000 units.

In 1972, Ford promoted new colors and fabrics, the prettiest of which was the Sprint decor option, available for hardtop and SportsRoof models. It could be combined with mag wheels, raised white-letter tires and, competition suspension. On the outside, Sprints were usually painted white and had broad, blue Shelby-style racing stripes edged with red. Complementary colors were used inside. "Control and balance make it a beautiful experience," the ads read.

By this time, of course, Ford was well on its way to designing a totally new Mustang—a car that would be more faithful to the spirit of the original. Typically, the real push for a total redesign came from president Lee A. Iacocca. "I've said it a hundred times and I'll say it again: The Mustang market never left us, we left it," Iacocca would remark later. "We kept the 460-cid

This 1973 Mustang convertible wears an optional hood similar to the Mach I's.

1973 Mustang Grande

1973 Mach I

engine out of it, but we had all the other engines in it." Echoed vice president for design Eugene Bordinat: "We started out with a secretary car and all of a sudden we had a behemoth."

For one more year, in 1973, the Mustang remained its hefty self and slightly more units were sold than in 1972. Convertible sales scored the largest percentage increase—up 100 percent to nearly 12,000 units—because Ford had announced the convertibles would be discontinued the next year. The 1973 Mustang convertible was the last ragtop Ford built.

Meanwhile, the federal government had issued its impact standards for bumpers that would now have to sustain low-speed front and rear shunts without damage. To meet this requirement, many auto makers, including Ford, designed some pretty awful looking cowcatchers. The Mustang fared rather well since the '73 bumper stuck out only a little more than in '72 and didn't look too bad. The bumper consisted of an I-beam mounting bar inside a box-section bracket. This assembly was attached to two longitudinal rubber blocks which gave way on contact, then bounced back to their original position. An optional color-keyed rubber cover was available to clean up appearance even more. It was a costly but reasonable solution to what seemed like an unreasonable mandate.

The influence of other federal requirements was evident too. The 1973 dash panel was restyled to eliminate sharp control knobs and other projections that might cause unnecessary injury in a crash and got extra padding. Bigger brakes were used, as were larger calipers for cars with non-power discs. Flame-retardant materials were used to meet the government's "burn rate" of four inches per minute. Emission control was handled by crankcase ventilation and exhaust gas recirculation. The EGR system routed gases from the exhaust manifold through a vacuum valve into the carburetor where they were diluted by the incoming fuel-air mixture. This permitted a leaner carburetor setting and lower emissions.

Except for the front bumper, the 1973 Mustang was little changed from 1971-72. Mustang was the only '73 Ford car to feature an optional 351 High-Output engine. Prices, which had been cut to spark sales the year before, remained fairly stable. The base six-cylinder hardtop listed at $2,760 while the V-8 convertible was the most expensive Mustang at $3,189. The Mach 1, which came with 351-cid, 162 (net) hp engine as standard, sold for $3,088.

Nine years after the first Mustang's debut, the old marketing technique of offering a wide range of options was still important. The '73, Ford said, was "designed to be designed by you." Mustang's optional vinyl roof now came in six colors. It covered the whole roof on hardtops and the front three-quarters on fastbacks. A hood with lock pins and matte silver or black-colored center section was available. Also on the list were forged aluminum wheels, "metallic glow" paint, and decorative side striping. Convertibles and hardtops could be ordered with black-finish grilles which contained auxiliary spotlamps. An electric rear window defroster was available on hardtops and SportsRoofs.

Thus ended the last of the first-generation Mustang ponycars. Though its basic shape, sporty styling, and long option list remained, the Mustang had evolved into something completely different than the 1965 original. Everybody knew this, and by 1973 everybody also knew this wasn't the way to go. For 1974, Lee Iacocca was planning a whole new product: The Mustang II would be a second revolution.

Specifications

Model Year Production

No.	Model	1971	1972	1973
63D	Fastback, standard	23,956	15,622	10,820
63R	Fastback, Mach 1	36,499	27,675	35,440
65D	Hardtop, standard	65,696	57,350	51,480
65F	Hardtop, Grande	17,406	18,045	25,674
76D	Convertible, standard	6,121	6,401	11,853
	TOTAL	149,678	125,093	134,867

Prices/Weights

Models	1971	1972	1973
01 hardtop, 6	$2,911/2,937	$2,729/2,941	$2,760/2,995
02 fastback, 6	$2,973/2,907	$2,786/2,908	$2,820/3,008
03 convertible, 6	$3,227/3,059	$3,015/3,051	$3,102/3,126
04 Grande, 6	$3,117/2,963	$2,915/2,965	$2,946/3,003
01 hardtop, V-8	$3,006/3,026	$2,816/3,025	$2,897/3,085
02 fastback, V-8	$3,068/2,993	$2,873/2,995	$2,907/3,098
02 Boss 302, V-8	$4,124/3,281	—	—
03 convertible, V-8	$3,320/3,145	$3,101/3,147	$3,189/3,216
04 Grande, V-8	$3,212/3,049	$3,002/3,051	$3,088/3,115
05 Mach 1, V-8	$3,268/3,220	$3,053/3,046	$3,088/3,115

General Specifications	1971	1972	1973
Wheelbase:	109.0	109.0	109.0
Overall length:	187.5(6) 189.5(8)	190.0	194.0
Overall width:	75.0	75.0	75.0
Std. Trans.:	3-speed manual	3-speed manual	3-speed manual
Optional Trans.:	4-speed manual 3-speed automatic	4-speed manual 3-speed automatic	4-speed manual 3-speed automatic

Engine Availability

Type	CID	HP	1971	1972	1973
I-6	250	145 (gross)[a]	Std.	Std.	Std.
V-8	302	220 (gross)[b]	Std.	Std.	Std.
V-8	302	285 (gross)	Opt.	—	—
V-8	429	370 (gross)	Opt.	—	
V-8	351	330 (gross)	Std.[c]	—	—
V-8	351	162 (net)	—	Opt.	Opt.[d]
V-8	351	200 (net)	—	Opt.	Opt.
V-8	351	223 (net)	—	Opt.	Opt.

a: rated 98hp (net) 1972; 99hp (net) 1973
b: rated 142hp (net) 1972; 136hp (net) 1973
c: Std. Boss 351 only
d: Std. Mach I

The Second Revolution: 1974

The smaller and lighter Mustang II was a major turning point in the marque's history—a second revolution. Its introduction couldn't have been better timed. The all-new car arrived in Ford showrooms almost simultaneously with the Arab oil embargo of 1973-74—and people flocked to those showrooms in droves. With a production run of 385,993 units in its first year, the Mustang II came within ten percent of the original Mustang's 12-month record of 418,812 cars. Lee Iacocca was behind it—again—and those first-year sales made Iacocca look pretty good—again. Of course, the Mustang II was being developed years before the Arabs decided to put the squeeze on oil

supplies. That they did this so soon after the car was introduced was simply mere coincidence.

Changes in the market since the original Mustang appeared were already apparent in some recent Dearborn products. The Ford Maverick, introduced in 1970, was dimensionally close to the 1965 Mustang. In its first year, the Maverick topped the Mustang's first-year sales record with over 450,000 units. But the Maverick was not the sporty car the first Mustang had been. The Mustang II was designed to fill that role.

While Iacocca had only guessed that a market for the original Mustang existed, this time he knew *in advance* there would be demand for the Mustang II.

This smooth proposal for 1974 was shown in late '71.

Grille was already much like '74 shape.

The styling influence of Ford's European branches is evident in this car's clean, simple lines.

Another late-'71 study looks like a two-seater.

Chunky lines and side windows recall Italian exotics.

Sporty imports—2 + 2 coupes with luxurious interiors, bucket seats, and four-speed gearboxes—were becoming increasingly popular. Ford's Capri and GM's Opel Manta (both "captive imports") plus the Toyota Celica and the Datsun PL610 were selling wonderfully well. In 1965, such sporty coupes accounted for less than 100,000 units. But by 1972, they were up to 300,000 and projections for 1974 put sales at over 400,000. Part of the Mustang II's objective was to capture a big slice of this pie.

Ford design vice-president Eugene Bordinat gave full credit for the Mustang II's concept to the father of the original Mustang: "Iacocca was the first guy to come along who had the feeling for cars that had existed in General Motors for some time." Said Iacocca: "When I look at the foreign car market and see that one in five is a sporty car, I know something's happening. Look at what the Celica started to do before the two devaluations (of the dollar) nailed it! Anyone who decides to sit this out just ain't gonna dance!"

Once again, Dearborn's mighty army of stylists and engineers concentrated their attention on Mustang. As before, they worked from an idea clearly defined by Iacocca: "The new Mustang must be small—with a wheelbase between 96 and 100 inches. It must be a sporty notchback and/or coupe—the convertible is

dead and can be forgotten. It must come as standard with a four-speed manual gearbox, and a four-cylinder or small six-cylinder engine. Most important it must be luxurious—upholstered in quality materials, and carefully built." Ben Bidwell, who handled Mustang II product planning, said Iacocca took a personal interest in the quality control aspect: "He will be out there in the showroom and he'll run his finger around the molding, and if it so much as scrapes him some poor son of a gun will get it."

The Mustang II's flashy interior was created by David Ash of Ford Design. Ash said he was partly inspired by Jaguar, Rolls-Royce, and Mercedes. To give his prototype interior the feel of that in a real automobile, Ash built a complete interior mockup—an unusual procedure in the design business. It had exterior sheet metal and all four wheels attached. "It was a time-consuming thing to build," Ash said, "but it served its purpose very well. We didn't have to go through an elaborate series of meetings to determine everything. It was all approved right there. We were on a crash basis to get it done, and it was very enthusiastically received. . . We put everything in that we could conceive of that connotes restrained elegance plus the get-up-and-go that says Mustang—something of a fire breather . . . It's a kind of a mini-T-Bird."

The Mustang II's dashboard was dominated by a

This formal roof fastback was considered for 1975.

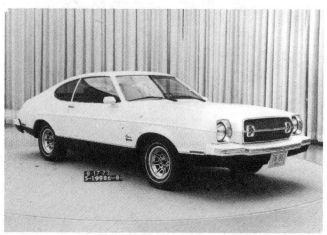

Ford also considered a Capri version of '74 Mustang.

large oblong panel placed squarely in front of the driver and housing all controls and instruments, which surprisingly included a tachometer, temperature gauge, and ammeter as standard. The seats were upholstered in pleated cloth, vinyl, or optional leather—very plush. There was no seatback rake adjustment, sad to say, but the seats themselves were definitely more comfortable than those of any previous Mustang. Rear seat legroom was limited because the Mustang II was seen primarily as a car for two adults in the front. There was enough room in the back for a couple of small children, or an adult passenger could be comfortable there for a short period of time.

On the outside, the long-hood, short-deck proportions were retained but on a reduced scale—smaller than even the original Mustang. The real target was to match the dimensions of the imported sporty subcompacts. Compare the measurements, for example, of the 1965 Mustang, the Mustang II, and the 1974 Toyota Celica:

Dimension (")	Mustang	Mustang II	Celica
Wheelbase	108.0	96.2	95.5
Length	181.6	175.0	163.9
Width	70.2	68.2	63.0
Height	51.0	49.9	51.6

Compared to the 1973 Mustang, the "II" was 20 inches shorter, four inches narrower, an inch lower, and some 400 to 500 pounds lighter. Its wheelbase was nearly 13 inches less than the 1973 version's.

At announcement time, some observers suggested that the Mustang II was really just a Pinto with a sporty body. That reasoning is not completely accurate. Although the two cars shared many components, the 1974 Pinto was actually upgraded over previous editions by using some parts and features designed for the Mustang II.

Both Pinto and Mustang II were unit-body cars. Their front suspension was the same: independent with unequal-length upper and lower arms and coil springs. On the Mustang, the lower arm was attached to a rubber-mounted subframe; on the Pinto it was bolted directly to the body structure. The Mustang subframe carried the rear of the engine/transmission assembly and was designed to provide more precise steering and a smoother ride than the Pinto offered. Isolating the rear engine mount from the main body structure helped keep drivetrain vibration from being transmitted to the passenger compartment. Mustang II was intended to sell at a higher price than the Pinto, so the Ford cost accountants approved this more expensive engine mounting arrangement.

Both the 1974 Pinto and Mustang II had rack-and-pinion steering but the Mustang's steering gear was mounted differently, again to minimize shock. The Mustang (but not the Pinto) could also be ordered with power steering.

At the rear, Mustang's leaf springs were two inches longer than Pinto's and its shock absorbers were staggered, as in the earlier high-performance Mus-

1974 Mustang II Ghia hardtop

1974 Mustang II hatchback

1974 Mustang II Mach I

1974 Mustang II Ghia hardtop

tangs. Spring rates were calculated by computers to match the equipment, weight, and body style of each individual car. The Ghia notchback, for example, came with very soft settings, while the optional competition suspension had the highest spring rates, along with a thicker front sway bar, a rear sway bar, and Gabriel adjustable shock absorbers.

The Mustang II body was a collection of styling ideas taken from several design proposals developed independently by the Ford and Lincoln-Mercury studios and the Italian coachbuilding firm of Ghia (which had recently been purchased by Ford). The final decision came down to a choice of five clay models, one notchback and four fastbacks. The one selected as the basis for the production styling was done by Lincoln-Mercury. Mustang II styling got a mixed reception. Some felt the notchback was a hodge-podge. The three-door fastback coupe was considered more handsome but it was not a "classic" shape like the '65

Mustang. If Mustang IIs ever become collector's items, the Mach I fastbacks will very likely be the most highly prized.

For the first time in Mustang's history, the model range was planned without a V-8 engine. In '74, the Mustang II's engine offerings were a 2.3-liter inline four and a 2.8-liter single overhead camshaft V-6. The four was the first American-built engine based on metric measurements, which is not surprising. Originally designed for some of Ford's larger European cars, (including the German and British Capri), the 2.3-liter unit was actually a bored and stroked version of the European 2.0-liter engine already being used on the American Pinto. A novel feature was its "monolithic engine timing." After each engine was assembled, an electronic timing device hooked into a computer was connected to two sensors on the engine: an indicator point at the rear of the crankshaft and an electrical terminal between the distributor and coil. The computer

Stallion trim was offered on 1976 Mustang II hatchback.

Stripes on 1976 Cobra II were inspired by Shelby-Mustang.

1977 Mustang II hatchback

Cobra II was available in more colors for 1977.

Note sunroof and wire wheel covers on '78 Mustang II.

The 1978 Mach I with optional T-roof

compared readings from each sensor and then set timing automatically by means of a distributor adjustment. Because the computer could set timing very precisely, this technique was very useful for meeting the increasingly tough engine emission standards.

The Mustang II's V-6 used the camshaft, valve train, pushrods, and distributor from the European version of this engine, but was modified in other ways. It was bored and stroked to increase capacity from 2.6 liters to 2.8 liters. It also had separate (instead of siamesed) exhaust ports for performance and good thermal qualities. Dual exhausts were standard. The V-6 could be ordered as an option on any Mustang but was standard on the Mach I three-door hatchback. Like the first Pinto engines the V-6 was built overseas at Ford's plant in Cologne, West Germany.

The Mustang II's standard four-speed gearbox was based on the British four-speed unit used also in the Pinto, but was strengthened to handle the Mustang's more powerful engines. The vacuum-assisted brakes were a combination of 9.3-inch discs up front and 9x1.75-inch drums in the rear.

Standard Mustang IIs, and especially Ghia models, were typically American in ride and handling. The Mach I with its standard V-6, radial tires, and optional competition suspension was a more capable road car. No Mustang II was overwhelming in acceleration. For its size the car had a rather high curb weight of 2,650-2,900 pounds. A V-6 car with four-speed would produce 0-to-60 mph times in the 13-14 second range and a top speed of around 100 mph.

The Mustang II didn't change significantly during its five years in production. Ghia notchbacks in both four-cylinder and V-6 form as well as the V-6-only Mach I were available for the full five-year run. Ford continued its tradition of offering a lengthy list of options. Aside from air conditioning and a variety of radios and tape players, the 1974 Mustang II could be ordered with a vinyl top, sunroof, and forged aluminum wheels, among other items. In 1975, Ford added an extra-cost flip-up glass "moonroof" at $454, and a "luxury package" for the already posh Ghia.

The Mustang II did not sell as well after 1974. Sales were down by over half for the 1975 model year. But after that production held steady with about 190,000 cars being sold each year. This was certainly more desirable and more profitable for Ford considering Mustang's sales in the early '70s.

Emission and safety regulations notwithstanding, a small but enthusiastic group of Mustang buyers still craved performance. Ford catered to these people by reviving the V-8 engine as an option for 1975. This was the familiar 302-cid unit tuned to deliver 122 net horsepower; that increased to 139 hp in 1976.

Since the Mustang V-8 displaced about 5.0-liters (metrically speaking), and the Chevrolet Monza 2+2 offered a 4.3-liter V-8, it was natural to make comparisons. The editors at *Road & Track* clearly preferred the Monza. And, despite the subjective judgements involved, they were probably right. In 1975, the brand-new Monza was a fresh, modern design that seemed

1978 Mustang II Ghia hardtop

King Cobra option appeared for 1978.

smoother and more integrated than the Mustang II. The Monza's comfort, ride, handling, and fuel economy were all judged to be better than the Ford's.

Road & Track summed up the feeling of many by saying the Mustang II's styling was "humpy and bumpy, and—in its interior—downright garish." Its interior, *R&T* felt, lacked "ergonomic refinement." The Mustang beat the Monza in acceleration by a healthy margin, as one would expect with a larger displacement engine—but it used a lot more gas. The only big advantage the Mustang II seemed to have was in braking. Here are *R&T's* test results:

Test Results	Mustang II	Monza 2+2
engine CID/bhp/rpm	302/122/3600	262/110/3600
0-to-60 mph, sec.	10.5	13.4
¼-mile, speed/sec.	77.0/17.9	72.5/19.5
top speed, mph	106	103
fuel economy, mpg	13.0	17.0

In further pursuit of sport—or what was left of it—Ford offered the Cobra II for 1976. This was basically a trim option available on the three-door only and included a sports steering wheel, dual remote-control outside mirrors, brushed aluminum appliques on dash and door panels, and Cobra II door trim. The exterior featured a blacked-out grille, styled steel wheels with trim rings, radial tires, flip-type quarter windows with louvers, front air dam, rear spoiler, and simulated hood scoop. Other decorative touches included Cobra II identification on the rocker panels, grille, and fenders. Cobra IIs were offered only in white with blue striping in 1976, but were available in other color combinations beginning in 1977. They were flashy, but a far cry from the Mach I, the Boss 302, or the Shelby-Mustangs (which inspired the Cobra II's blue-and-white color scheme).

A special option for the 1977 Ghia model was the "Sports Appearance Group" available with black or tan paintwork only. The package included many color-coordinated components in black or tan, including a console, three-spoke sports steering wheel, cast aluminum wheels with chamois-color spokes, and a trunk luggage rack with hold-down straps and bright buckles.

In 1978, Ford again tried "paint-on performance" with the King Cobra option. Like the Cobra II package (which was continued), the King Cobra kit was available only on the three-door fastback and had every racy styling touch any kid could want. There was a snake decal on the hood and tape stripes on the roof, rear deck, rocker panels, and "A" pillar, around the wheel wells, and on the air dam which was also part of the package. The words "King Cobra" appeared on each door and on the standard decklid spoiler. A black-finished grille, window moldings, headlamp bezels, and wiper arms, plus a brushed-aluminum instrument panel applique completed the package. King

Cobras were fitted with the 302-cid V-8, power steering, "Rallye" handling package, and Goodrich 70-series T/A raised white-letter radial tires. Given all that bold advertising, this was the least Ford could do. And it's probably true that the King Cobra's 17-second quarter-mile time was considered high performance by 1978 standards.

Aside from variable-ratio power steering, electronic voltage regulator, optional "Wilshire" cloth for the Ghia, and a reshuffle of paint and upholstery colors, the 1978 Mustang II was pretty much like the earlier versions. It still sold reasonably well. Model year sales of 192,000 units were second only to the introduction year of 1974. Actually, 1978 production would have been higher but some early '78s were delivered to dealers earlier than usual because of low inventory and were registered as '77s.

But it was clearly time for a new approach and new ideas—a Mustang for the 1980s. The Mustang II had been around for five years and had served its purpose. As in earlier times, Lee Iacocca once again poured over market projections, buyer surveys, and government requirements, searching for a formula that would again make Mustang a winner in 1979 and beyond. A new generation was on the way.

Specifications

Model Year Production

No.	Model	1974	1975	1976	1977*	1978
60F	Standard, 2dr	177,671	85,155	78,508	67,783	81,304
60H	Ghia, 2dr	89,477	52,320	37,515	29,510	34,730
69F	Standard, 3dr	74,799	30,038	62,312	49,161	68,408
69R	Mach 1, 3dr	44,046	21,062	9,232	6,719	7,968
	TOTAL	385,993	188,575	187,567	153,173	192,410

* 1977 figure includes vehicles produced as 1978 models but sold as 1977 models.

Prices/Weights

Models	1974	1975	1976	1977	1978
02 2dr, 4	$3,134/2,620	$3,529/2,660	$3,525/2,678	$3,702/2,627	$3,731/2,608
03 3dr, 4	$3,328/2,699	$3,818/2,697	$3,781/2,706	$3,901/2,672	$3,975/2,654
04 Ghia 2dr, 4	$3,480/2,886	$3,938/2,704	$3,859/2,729	$4,119/2,667	$4,149/2,646
02 2dr, V-6	$3,363/2,689	$3,801/2,775	$3,791/2,756	$3,984/2,750	$3,944/2,705
03 3dr, V-8	$3,557/2,768	$4,090/2,812	$4,047/2,784	$4,183/2,795	$4,188/2,751
04 Ghia 2dr, V-6	$3,709/2,755	$4,210/2,819	$4,125/2,807	$4,401/2,790	$4,362/2,743
05 Mach 1, V-6	$3,674/2,778	$4,188/2,879	$4,209/2,822	$4,332/2,785	$4,430/2,733

General Specifications	1974	1975	1976	1977	1978
Wheelbase:	96.2	96.2	96.2	96.2	96.2
Overall length:	175.0	175.0	175.0	175.0	175.0
Overall width:	70.2	70.2	70.2	70.2	70.2
Std. Trans.:	4-speed manual	4-speed manual	4-speed manual	4-speed manual	4-speed manual
Optional Trans.:	3-speed automatic	3-speed automatic	3-speed automatic	3-speed automatic	3-speed automatic

Engine Availability

Type	CID	HP	1974	1975	1976	1977	1978
I-4	140	a	Std.	Std.	Std.	Std.	Std.
V-6	171	b	Opt.d	Opt.	Opt.	Opt.	Opt.
V-8	302	c	—	Opt.	Opt.	Opt.	Opt.

a: rated 85hp 1974; 83hp 1975; 92hp 1976; 89hp 1977; 88hp 1978   c: rated 122hp 1975; 139hp 1976-78
b: rated 105hp 1974; 97hp 1975; 103hp 1976; 93hp 1977; 90hp 1978   d: Standard Mach I

Driving Impressions:
1974 Mustang II Mach I

One of the contributors to this book drove the Mach I version of the Mustang II in Detroit shortly after its introduction. The following impressions are based on notes from that test drive. It should be noted the car was driven by the owner—then and now—of an Opel Manta Luxus. This was one of the sporty subcompacts Lee Iacocca spoke of as Mustang II's target.

In our opinion, the Mustang II did not fully reply to competition from imports like the Manta Luxus. It was, after all, intended to appeal to the American public, which dictated certain "mass market" characteristics. The Manta handles and steers with more crispness and authority than the Mustang II. It is also more comfortable. Though the Mustang II we drove had a very plush interior, the luxury was more for the eye than for the seat of the pants. The Manta's cloth-upholstered contoured seats are adjustable for rake. The Mustang's pleated vinyl seats aren't. In the Manta passengers sit high, with excellent visibility in all directions. In the Mustang visibility is good, but the seating position is much lower and, typical of American cars, creates the impression of sitting in a bathtub.

Styling is a generally subjective matter, but to our eyes the Manta is a beautifully integrated design. Had BMW or Mercedes built a 2.0-liter subcompact, it would probably have looked like Opel's. The Mustang II, on the other hand, is a less unified design. To us, the front and rear seem to have been designed by two different committees.

Our Mach I had many of the optional extras offered in '74. With air conditioning, the "rallye package," power steering, and Ghia interior, it listed new at about $4,400, or about $700 above the base price. Our car also had the optional five-inch alloy wheels fitted with CR70x13 radial tires, which are wider than the standard BR70x13s. (Our Manta Luxus, incidentally, cost about $3,500 when new, equipped with air conditioning. The Opel had cord-type cloth interior and carpeting as standard. No special suspension was offered but the handling was already very good. It was not available with power steering either, and none was needed.)

The 1965 Mustang GT tested earlier in these pages weighs more than the Mustang II, but has a weight-to-

Our Mach I test car had lots of extras, including the optional alloy wheels.

Mustang II proved to be a good-handling car but the power steering lacked adequate feel.

Bucket seats need reclining adjustment for more comfort.

Dash layout is good, but minor gauges are hard to read.

horsepower ratio of only 16.5 pounds per (gross) horsepower. For the sake of comparison, (and converting the Mustang II's horsepower rating from net to gross figures), the '74 Mach I has a ratio of about 20 pounds per horsepower. That difference is significant. While our Mustang GT was anything but sluggish, the Mustang II felt definitely underpowered: It was slower by a fraction than the 1.9-liter Manta which had less horsepower but also less curb weight. A quarter-mile acceleration time on the average of 20 seconds at about 73 mph (indicated) hardly puts the Mach I in fast company. Such acceleration was even less than Ford's own V-6 Capri. On the other hand, the Mach I's V-6 engine was quiet and smooth-running at all speeds. We found it definitely quieter than the Capri, and about on a par with the Manta.

It seems, too, that Ford hadn't really licked the driveability problems of emission-controlled cars in the mid-'70s. Our Mustang II was extremely sluggish right after a cold start and the engine threatened to stall until it was completely warmed up. The throttle was difficult to control. A light touch on the pedal produced the

hesitant, jerky motion typical of lean surge. Pushing the pedal further to the floor resulted in smoother response, but at the expense of gas mileage. Mileage, incidentally, was a disappointment. Over 600 miles of moderate driving our Mach I returned only slightly more than 18 miles per gallon. (The Manta and Capri both did well over 20 mpg. Our Manta has consistently returned 25 mpg at a steady 55 mph; the Capri V-6 we drove in 1976 was about 2 mpg thirstier.)

The Mach I's cockpit leaves no doubt about the car's Detroit origins. The steering wheel is plastic (a vinyl-covered wheel was optional), and too large. The dashboard is a large cowled affair housing a small tachometer and speedometer. Three minor gauges offset to the lower right are even more tiny and are hard to read at a glance. The low driving position seems confining with a high center console on one side and a thick, high door panel on the other. The seats were fairly comfortable, but the lack of a reclining mechanism made it less easy to be comfortable than in cars like the Manta and Capri which have this feature. This particular Mach I had the Ghia luxury interior option

($96) which offered softer-than-standard vinyl upholstery, color-coordinated two-toning on seats and backrests, fake wood trim on the doors, European-style armrests with built-in grab handles, and heavier pile carpeting. So the only functional aspect of the Ghia interior is the armrests.

The Mustang II came standard with a Pinto-based four-speed all-synchromesh gearbox. Gear ratios were 3.65 in first, 1.97 in second, 1.37 in third, and 1.00 in fourth. The final drive ratio of 3.355:1 was higher numerically than the Capri's 3.22:1. Apparently the Mustang's gearing was selected to favor acceleration. We found the four-speed to be smooth and precise in operation, but third gear is a long reach away. The handbrake lever sits at an awkward 45-degree angle when the brake is fully on. A long hard tug is required before the handbrake takes hold and the lever is difficult to release because of its high angle.

The Mach I has an advantage over the Opel Manta in cargo capacity. Folding down the rear seatback opens up a 28 cubic-foot cargo space. Notchback Mustangs, however, have less than 10 cubic feet of space compared to the Manta's voluminous 15 cubic-foot trunk which, like the Mustang, is separated from the fixed back seat by a bulkhead.

While its acceleration was hardly of the pin-you-to-the-seat variety, we found the handling of our Mach I test car to be fairly good. Its suspension option (with the adjustable shocks at their hardest setting) kept the car from wallowing or floating without seriously effecting the notably smooth ride. Staggered rear shocks help keep the back end under control and there was little wheel hop even over bumpy surfaces. The power steering was very precise—far better than the standard manual steering—but lacked sufficient road feel. Our car's special radial-ply tires undoubtedly contributed to the good handling. (Radials were standard on all Mustang IIs, though the ones on our car were wider than stock.)

The Mach I's vacuum-assisted front disc-rear drum brake system worked extremely well. Pedal effort required for hard braking was not excessive, yet the system was not so overpowered that passengers would be sent through the windshield in a panic stop. The vacuum assist was an option. Contemporary road tests noted that the unassisted brakes required much heavier pedal effort.

Several interior features of our Mach I were particularly appreciated. One of these was its sensible seatbelt arrangement. To prevent the belts from becoming tangled, a common annoyance on many 1974 American cars, Ford used automatic retractor reels for both lap and shoulder belts, the latter equipped with an inertia lock. At the time of our test the Mach I's mandatory ignition interlock device was still hooked up and prevented the car from being started unless belts were fastened. Most owners of cars with interlock avoided this nuisance by simply clipping the wires. The interlock was soon dropped from the government's list of required safety equipment.

Another good feature of the Mustang II is its heating and ventilation. The air conditioning worked with all the smooth efficiency we have come to expect of Detroit units. Without the air conditioner, the ventilation system delivered a refreshing blast of cool air at face level. The heater also proved to be effective and powerful.

Our general impression of the Mustang II is that it met Lee Iacocca's design directives. It was not intended to be Dearborn's version of the Capri, because Ford did not want to compete directly with its own successful import. The Mustang II lacked the precision, balance, and handling refinement of cars like Capri, Manta, and Toyota Celica. On the other hand, it did offer a high level of quality in both construction and materials. It was luxurious, by Detroit's definition of that term, and it certainly appealed to many buyers of sporty subcompact coupes.

Specifications

	1974 Mustang II Mach I
Price when new:	$4,396
Engine type, cylinders:	ohc V-6
Bore x Stroke (in.):	3.66x2.70
Displacement (cu. in.):	171
Compression ratio:	8.2:1
Horsepower @ rpm:	105(net) @ 5200
Transmission type/forward gears:	manual/4
Final drive ratio:	3.55:1
Tire size:	CR70/x13
Steering, turns lock-to-lock:	3.3
Turning diameter (ft.):	34.0
Brake swept area (sq. in.):	244.0
Curb weight (lbs.):	2778
Weight distribution, front/rear:	57/43
Wheelbase (in.):	96.2
Overall length (in.):	175.0
Overall width (in.):	70.2
Track, front/rear (in.):	55.6/55.8
Height (in.):	49.6
Ground clearance (in.):	4.5
Suspension, front:	upper A-arms, lower lateral arms; coiled anti-roll bar; tube shocks
Suspension, rear:	live axle; semi-elliptic leaf springs; anti-roll bar; tube shocks
Performance	
pounds/horsepower (net):	26.5
acceleration, 0-60 mph (sec.):	13.5
estimated top speed (mph):	100.0

Competition Mustangs: From B~Production to Trans~Am

Mustang competition began and ended with Carroll Shelby. The whole purpose of Shelby's program (see Chapter 7) was to create a genuine dual purpose race-and-ride sports car out of the basic Ford package. And the idea worked. The Shelby GT-350 dominated its class in SCCA (Sports Car Club of America) competition. Thanks to Shelby, Mustangs also made pretty fair showings in drag racing and in the Trans-Am sedan championship series.

The "Competition Prepared" GT-350 was stripped of all insulation, carpeting, door panels, and window operating mechanisms. The only glass it retained was the windshield. Plexiglass side windows in aluminum frames and a one-piece plexiglas rear window were used for the rest of the greenhouse. A one-piece fiberglass front apron replaced the front bumper and gravel pan. The apron had a large cutout in its center which ducted air to the oil cooler and two smaller holes for front brake cooling. The rear bumper, which on the first cars was painted white to match the body, was

A GT-350 (above) overtakes a Porsche 904 (below); Shelby-Mustangs dominated SCCA B-Production in '65 and '66.

The GT-350 (left) and GT40 (right) are shown during the 24-hour race at Daytona International Speedway in early 1966.

later left off entirely. A long-range 34-gallon gas tank was installed with a quick-release cap and a large splash tunnel. American Racing Equipment 7x15-inch five-spoke magnesium wheels were used exclusively on all racing GT-350s.

Even by racing standards, the interior of the competition model was stark. Almost everything was finished in semi-gloss black. The dash, from which all padding, the glove compartment, radio, and ashtray had been removed, was left with only an ignition switch, light and wiper switches, and a bank of "CS" competition gauges. From left to right, they monitored fuel pressure, oil temperature, speed (0-160 mph), revs (0-8000 rpm), oil pressure, and water temperature. Two light-weight fiberglass racing bucket seats padded in black vinyl were used. There were also three-inch competition lap-belts, a roll bar, and a fire extinguisher.

The "R" or competition-model engines were advertised as fully dyno-tuned and race ready. They developed between 325 and 350 gross horsepower.

Jerry Titus' GT-350 duels with XK-E at Riverside.

A competition '67 flashes past the crowd.

A hardtop heads into the turn at a regional race.

The competition-prepared Shelby-Mustangs could really fly.

A GT-350 leaves the track at Daytona.

Mustangs were strong competitors on the Daytona road course; car on right is a little off course.

The GT-350 had impressive win record in mid-'60s.

Titus drove this car for Shelby's Terlingua team.

The green flag drops and a GT-350 roars off toward another victory.

Beginning with the production 271-hp Hi-Performance 289 engine, Shelby balanced and blueprinted all components. Ports were enlarged, polished, and matched to the combustion chambers. Pistons were fly-cut and a special camshaft was installed. A high-volume oil pump, oil cooler, special tube headers backed by straight pipes, and special valve cover breathers were fitted. The racing carburetor was a 715 cfm Holley which gulped air through a spun-aluminum plenum chamber mated to the hood scoop. The gearbox was Borg-Warner's T-10 "Sebring" model supplied with both aluminum and cast iron cases. A steel plate competition clutch disc was fitted. Every R-model GT-350 was track-tested at Willow Springs Raceway prior to shipment.

The R-model listed for $5,950, a bargain price even for 1965. That, of course, was part of the Ford philosophy. Since 1962, the company had emphasized competition, in an attempt to add a performance image to its street machines.

Not only did the image-making work but the racing package itself was formidable. On Valentine's Day 1965, Shelby American served notice that the only time Corvettes would see Victory Circle was when there were no GT-350s entered. Duly certified for Class B-Production in SCCA, the Mustangs went rapidly to work. The GT-350's first appearance resulted in three class wins.

Shelby-Mustang dominance of B-Production wasn't quite universal. In 1965, when the SCCA awarded national championships on a divisional basis, one 327-engine Corvette eked out a win in the Southwest region. The rest of 1965—and all of 1966 and 1967—saw a Shelby-Mustang parade. Here are the statistics:

B-Production National Champions

1965	Central: Robert Johnson, GT-350
	Midwest: Brad Brooker, Kansas, Corvette/GT-350
	Northeast: Mark Donohue, New Jersey, GT-350
	Pacific: Jerry Titus, California, GT-350
	Southeast: Bill Floyd, South Carolina, GT-350
	Southwest: Zoltan Petrany, Texas, Corvette
1966	Walter Hane, Florida, GT-350
1967	Fred Van Buren, Mexico City GT-350

Another lesser-known Shelby-Mustang effort was the drag racing program in the National Hot Rod Association (NHRA). During May, 1965, some members of the GT-350 project began exploring the possibilities of campaigning a GT-350 in NHRA B/Sports Production races. An earlier Shelby effort, the "Dragonsnake" AC Cobra, had put that car in the public eye on drag strips across the country. It seemed logical that a properly set up GT-350 could do the same thing for the Mustang.

The first GT-350 drag car was consigned to the noted engine and racing car builder Bill Stroppe for evaluation and development. NHRA had approved the engine modifications deemed necessary: machine-ported cylinder heads, 1.63-inch exhaust and 1.88-inch intake valves, heavy-duty valve springs, drag headers, and complete balancing and blueprinting. But it was decided that Shelby's "customer" cars would be sold with the stock 306-hp engine. Full-tilt competition engines would be used for the "factory" cars and would be available to private owners as an option. Making the stock engine standard, Shelby decided, offered two advantages. First, the car could be sold at a lower list price; second, it would avoid creating hard feelings in any customer should he blow up an expensive full-specification factory-built engine.

The National Hot Rod Association approved a scattershield for the GT-350 placed in the trunk (mandatory because the car had solid lifters). A drag clutch and pressure plate were also certified. Approval meant that these parts could be installed and sold on the car as it left the factory, saving owners the time and expense of removing the engine or transmission to fit these parts later.

Other modifications developed as the Mustang drag racer took shape. Cure Ride 90/10 uplock shock absorbers were installed on the front, while Gabriel 50/50 downlock shocks were used at the rear. Stroppe designed a set of ladder-bar torque arms. Also used was a Hurst "Competition Plus" shifter. Stroppe checked every loophole in the NHRA and AHRA (American Hot Rod Association) regulations. Some of his proposed modifications didn't make it to the strip because they were not legal. These included lengthened front spindles, modified seat tracks, re-radiused rear wheels, and relocated front upper control arms. Stroppe even considered a Weber carburetor-equipped, roller-cam "Factory Experimental" model. But it never got past the bench-test stage.

The first drag racing GT-350 was completed and sold to a Shelby dealer in Lorain, Ohio in August, 1965. A second car was bought and run by Mel Burns Ford of Long Beach, California. The actual number of GT-350 drag cars is not known. In addition to the 1965 models, a few 1966s were similarly prepared.

Overshadowed by the GT-350's stunning success in SCCA "club" racing was the Trans-Am effort. Trans-Am is short for the Trans-American Sedan Championship, first run in 1966. Essentially, it was an offshoot of the SCCA's sedan class events. The Trans-Am attracted Mustangs, Barracudas, Falcons, Dodge Darts, and a host of under-2.0-liter cars. Trans-Am races were intended to be "mini-enduros" that ranged anywhere from 200 to 2,400 miles, or two to 24 hours, and thus required pit stops for fuel and tires. By the end of 1966, Trans-Am racing was one of the most popular series on the SCCA schedule, and many professional factory teams had entered. To make things more interesting, a Manufacturer's Trophy was offered to the maker whose cars won the most races. Driver ego took a back seat as each factory vied with its rivals to uphold its performance image.

Trans-Am rules were based on FIA Appendix J

Titus is trailed by Terlingua racing teammate.

A Mustang gets pre-race check at Daytona.

The late Peter Revson drove this Boss 302 in 1969.

Bud Moore prepared this Boss 302 for 1970 Trans-Am.

Warren Tope won 1971 A-sedan crown in SCCA.

Parnelli Jones drove this car at Daytona Trans-Am.

Mustangs competed in European events for 1966.

White Mustang won this 1967 race at Bridgehampton, NY.

specifications for Series Production Cars (Group 1) or Touring Cars (Group 2). These cars were limited to engine displacements between 2000 and 5000 cc, a maximum wheelbase of 116 inches, and minimal performance modifications. Since only four-seaters were allowed, the GT-350 could not be used because it was officially a two-seat car. In its place, the Mustang notchback hardtop was pressed into service.

The 1966 schedule had seven races but the winner wasn't decided until the last race at Riverside, California—the series was that close all season. But it was at Riverside that a huge blue Shelby American race van appeared with a Shelby-ized notchback Mustang for Jerry Titus, editor of *Sports Car Graphic* and a former GT-350 team driver. Titus took the pole position in qualifying laps, and ultimately won the race which gave the Manufacturer's Trophy to Ford for 1966.

The eleventh-hour appearance of Shelby American signaled a change in Ford racing priorities, probably because everyone realized that the 1967 GT-350 would not be as competitive as the older R-models. The factory's Trans-Am effort would now have to be carried out with Mustang notchbacks.

Earlier in the season, Shelby American had permitted Mustang sedan competitors to participate in its race assistance program because the notchbacks shared virtually all mechanical components with the GT-350s. This offer of support was later withdrawn because it was felt that there was not enough product identification between the Shelbys and the stock notchback "sedans." Ford took up the slack by offering limited factory support to outstanding teams. By the end of the season both Ford and Shelby-American were committed to Trans-Am.

Not wanting to let its 1966 championship seem like a fluke, Ford sponsored a full-fledged two-car victory team put together by Shelby American. The canary yellow Mustang notchbacks with flat black hoods ran under the banner of "Terlingua Racing Team," an honorary team composed of "sponsors" of Shelby's Terlingua (Texas) Boys' Ranch.

The 1967 Trans-Am saw other factory teams running new model ponycars. A team of racing Cougars was fielded by stock car ace Bud Moore. Camaros, prepared by Roger Penske, were piloted by former GT-350 driver Mark Donohue. Other well-known drivers in 1967 were Dan Gurney, Parnelli Jones, George Follmer, Peter Revson, David Pearson, Ronnie Bucknum, and Jerry Titus. The '67 season was extended to 13 races. Shelby American's Mustang notchback crossed the finish lines often enough to pick up the trophy for a second year. Interestingly, most of Ford's attention that season was paid to the Bud Moore Cougars. They received more financial consideration than other Ford teams, plus "trick" parts and drivers Gurney and Jones. Despite that, Shelby American came home first.

By 1968, Group 2 rules were becoming difficult to manage, so they were bent slightly. All engines were allowed to be bored out to a limit of 5.0-liters (306 cubic inches). A minimum weight of 2,800 pounds was set,

and wheel rims up to eight inches wide could be used. The schedule again included 13 races. Shelby's Mustangs and Penske's Camaros were joined by a pair of factory-backed AMC Javelins, while the Cougar bowed out.

The 1968 Shelby Trans-Am racers were painted blue or red with flat black hoods, and ran under the "Shelby Racing Co." banner. Titus, still the lead Shelby driver, finished first in the initial 24-hour event at Daytona. But by the second race, the Penske/Donohue Camaro team started to click. They won races 2 through 9 before Titus broke the string at Watkins Glen. By that time there was no catching the Camaro, and it went on to take the 1968 championship.

By the first race of 1969, rules for Trans-Am cars differed even more from those governing Group 2 sedans. Mustang fastbacks were now legal and the new Boss 302 was the hot ticket. Shelby's team prepared a pair of these to compete in the 12-race schedule. The cars were driven by Peter Revson and Horst Kwech. A second Boss 302 team, fielded by Bud Moore, had Parnelli Jones and George Follmer in the driver's seats. Massive factory engineering efforts now produced semi-tube frame chassis (thinly disguised as roll cages), acid-dipped bodies, huge tires, flared fenders, spoilers, wings, and mind-boggling horsepower. The Boss 302 canted-valve engine made an impressive debut in the first race of the season. After a post-race check of lap charts, Parnelli Jones' Bud Moore Mustang was declared the winner.

The second race, at Lime Rock, Connecticut was won by Sam Posey in a Shelby-prepared Boss 302. That was the Shelby team's only victory that year. At Riverside on October 4, 1969, Carroll Shelby announced his retirement from racing.

Trans-Am racing reached its peak during the 1970 season. Despite the absence of the Shelby team, there were at least a half-dozen other big league entries: Penske Javelins, Bud Moore Boss 302 Mustangs, Jim Hall's Chaparral Camaros, Jerry Titus' Firebirds, Dan Gurney's Barracudas and Dodge Challengers, and the Owens/Corning Camaros. The Mustang was Trans-Am champion once again in 1970, besting all its impressive rivals.

After 1970, the factories began to withdraw their support, possibly because they had created an overwhelming amount of competition. In place of the factory teams more and more independents began to enter, but as they quickly learned, the price of being competitive was astronomical. Also, Detroit's ponycars had begun to increase in size and weight and foreign makes like Porsche, Alfa Romeo, and Datsun had started to win races regularly. In a desperate attempt to attract the large crowds of 1970, SCCA allowed A-Production, B-Production, and A-Sedan cars to compete in the 1971 Trans-Am series: Corvettes, Camaros, Datsun Zs—even Cobras and GT-350s. But the electricity and excitement of earlier seasons had all but disappeared. The Trans-Am had come and gone, but the Mustang and Shelby American had been an exciting part of it.

The Third Revolution: 1979

When it first appeared, the 1979 Mustang may have fooled some people into thinking it was a new BMW. Its clean, taut, tight appearance was crisp and solid-looking. Its surface execution, downswept nose, ample glass area, and lack of ornamentation combined the best thinking of American and European stylists. Those who got close enough to see the familiar Mustang nameplate must have been impressed. At long last, Ford had created the kind of restrained, efficient, and elegant sporty car it set out to build in the first place.

Since then, owners of the '79 models have had little reason to change their favorable first impressions. Of course, the '79 inherited some of the Mustang's perennial problems: The handling is still far from perfect; the seats are too low; and there's a feeling of being hemmed in by the massive doors. The quality of the body construction also does not seem as good as

This is one of many proposals for '79 styling.

Many variations of this idea were worked up.

Roofline and rear fenders of this June, 1975 proposal resemble 1977 Thunderbird.

on most European competitors like the Volkswagen Scirocco, for example. Whether Detroit deliberately builds cars this "looser" way or whether it is simply the result of American production methods isn't important. No car, and especially one that has the Mustang's comparatively low price, can be faultless. By almost any standard, the '79 Mustang was still one of the most attractive buys ever offered.

As in the case of the Mustang II and most other recent Ford products, the 1979 Mustang's final shape was selected from a variety of proposals. Several styling teams within the Ford Motor Company were given the same design parameters from which they developed sketches, clay models, and fiberglass mock-ups. Quarter-scale clay models were tested for 136 hours in wind tunnels, because aerodynamics were becoming increasingly important to automobile design. Finally, finished fiberglass models were shown to top management. The winning entry was created by a team headed by Jack Telnack, executive director of Ford North American Light Truck and Car Design.

Telnack's group had also designed the styling study that went on to become the pretty little Ford Fiesta.

The design parameters given to Telnack's group and the others were set down by management in 1976. The new Mustang was to be built on the floorpan of the just-completed Ford Fairmont/Mercury Zephyr compact sedans. It could be shortened somewhat, and for Telnack's Mustang proposal it was—by 5.1 inches. The power units used in Mustang II—four, V-6, and 302 V-8—would be retained. As with the original Mustang, the car was pegged at a low curb weight—about 2,700 pounds. It was supposed to hold two adults comfortably, and four in a pinch. Like the original Mustang (but unlike the Mustang II) the notchback was styled first and the fastback developed afterward from it. Several trim versions were to be offered: standard, Sport Option, Ghia and Cobra. The latter had blacked-out greenhouse trim, black lower bodysides, color-keyed body moldings, and a snake design for the hood. (This last item, thankfully, could be deleted on request.)

Note Mercedes 450SLC-like ribbing on lower body of this September, 1975 design.

A rounded look was tried for '79 styling.

Square-cut contours were also contemplated.

A parade of prototypes for the '79 model contrasts with then-current Mustang II (left).

By 1976, a styling theme was emerging.

Ghia name and opera window appeared on this proposal.

There's a touch of Barracuda in this clay model.

This shape was still a long way from final '79 styling.

A T-Bird roofline was also considered for Mustang.

Another early 1976 study resembles Mustang II.

Telnack described the design project to the press in June 1978: "One of the basic themes for this car was 'form follows function'. . . and we wanted to be as aerodynamically correct as possible before getting into the wind tunnel. In the past we have designed cars and then gone into the tunnel mainly for tuning the major surfaces that have been approved on the car. With the Mustang the designers were thinking about aerodynamics in the initial sketch stages, which made the tuning job in the tunnel much easier. Consequently we wound up with the most slippery car ever done in the Ford Motor Company: A drag coefficient of 0.44 for the three-door fastback, 0.46 for the two-door notchback. (Aerodynamics is) probably the most cost-effective way to improve corporate average fuel economy. We know that a 10 percent improvement in drag can result in a five percent improvement in fuel economy at a steady-state 50 mph . . . That's really worthwhile stuff for us to go after."

Telnack's team included light car design manager Fritz Mayhew, pre-production design executive David Rees, and pre-production designer Gary Haas. The shape that evolved from their work was a sort of notchback wedge. It was very slim in the front, with a sharply sloped hood and a rather high cowl. The Mustang cowl was actually an inch higher than that of the Fairmont/Zephyr. Telnack said this was to "get a faster sloping hood and . . . to pivot the hood over the air cleaner." The shape required special inner front fender aprons and radiator supports instead of Zephyr/Fairmont components, but everyone agreed that the extra expense of these parts was warranted. Increased fuel economy was the reward. The front bumper with integrated spoiler and the slight lip on the rear decklid were also dictated by aerodynamic considerations. Both models had black finished slats behind the rear side windows, rather like those of the Mercedes 450SLC. The slats were perhaps too wide for optimum visibility—one of the new Mustang's less functional styling features.

The Mustang body used many lightweight components in place of heavier conventional ones wherever possible. The most common weight-saving materials used were plastics, high-strength low-alloy (HSLA) steel, and aluminum. The most significant use of plastics was for the reaction-injection-molded (RIM) soft urethane bumper covers. The number-three frame cross-member and the rear suspension arms were made of HSLA steel. Aluminum was found in the drivetrain and in the bumpers of some models. More weight was saved by the use of thin, but strong, glass and by thinner door design. The 1979 Mustangs weighed on the average about 200 pounds less than comparable Mustang IIs, though the newer cars were slightly larger in every dimension. In an age of downsizing, this bigger-but-lighter car was a remarkable achievement.

Careful attention was paid to the interior where many noticeable changes were made—most of them for the better. The "luxury" interiors were distinguished mainly by their higher quality materials. The '79 Ghia was less

Scale models of the '79 were wind tunnel tested.

Optional console with graphic display and digital clock

flashy than its '78 counterpart.

With more efficient use of available space, the '79 interior was far more roomy, comfortable, and convenient than the Mustang II's and sizeable gains were made in several key dimensions. Rear legroom was increased by over five inches. Overall interior volume was up by 14 cubic feet on the two-door notchback and 16 cubic feet on the hatchback. Thinner door construction yielded an improvement of 3.6 inches in front shoulder room and 2.0 inches in front hiproom. In the rear, these increases were 5.0 and 6.0 inches respectively. Cargo volume was likewise increased: Compared to the Mustang II, the '79 notchback offered two more cubic feet of trunk space, and the hatchback had four more cubic feet.

Many interior features of the '79 model were copied from European design practice. Full instrumentation—

1979 Mustang Ghia hardtop

Note Mercedes influence in rear window treatment.

1979 Mustang hatchback in Cobra trim

These snazzy wheels are part of TRX suspension.

Standard hardtop with lower bodyside moldings

This V-8 hardtop has "5.0" badge on front fender.

1979 Mustang hatchback

The Cobra hatchback and the Ghia hardtop

84

speedometer, trip odometer, tachometer, temperature gauge, oil pressure gauge, ammeter and fuel gauge— was standard. Two finger-tip stalks, one on each side of the steering column, controlled (on the left) the turn signals, headlight dimmer, and horn, and (on the right) the windshield wiper/washer. A third lever was added for adjusting the optional tilt steering wheel. Practical interior options were intermittent wipers, cruise control, and a console complete with graphic display for "vehicle systems monitoring." This display showed a silhouette of the car on which warning lights were appropriately placed to indicate low fuel; low windshield washer fluid; and failed headlights, taillights, or brake lights. The display could be tested by a pushbutton. The console also housed a quartz-crystal digital chronometer which showed time, date, or elapsed time at the touch of a button.

As with past Mustangs, the '79 version was designed to appeal to a broad market spectrum. According to Ford Division marketing plans manager Michael Woods, "Not too long ago we did a concept study on positioning the (imported) Capri and brought in imported car owners, some Capri owners, people who own small specialty cars. We showed them the (new Mustang) and talked to them about strategy. We were pretty gratified that an awful lot of people who were interested in the Capri felt that we had maintained the Capri theme—the functional styling of the car—and that it was consistent with the original car."

Now the German Ford Capri, especially in its larger-engine forms, was a very competent touring car. If the Mustang was to have a similar character its specifications would have to be greatly altered. Capri fans would not be satisfied with a plush, short-wheelbase coupe like the Mustang II that weighed too much and handled sluggishly. At the same time, Ford didn't want to lose the public which had bought Mustang IIs at the rate of 190,000 a year. From the suspension standpoint, therefore, several levels of performance had to be offered.

Ultimately, Ford planners settled on three suspensions: standard, "handling," and "special." Each was designed for—and issued with—its own set of tires. The standard suspension came with conventional bias-plys. The mid-level "handling" package used conventional radials. The special suspension used Michelin's recently developed TRX radials with a 390 mm diameter that required the use of specially sized wheels.

The basic suspension pieces came from the Fairmont/Zephyr sedans. The front suspension used MacPherson struts instead of conventional upper A-arms. Unlike the MacPherson arrangements found in most European and Japanese cars, the coil spring was not wrapped around the shock strut. Instead, it was mounted between the lower control arm and the vehicle structure. This eliminated the need for expensive tools like a spring compressor if the shocks needed to be replaced. A front anti-roll bar was standard on all cars, but its diameter varied according to the engine fitted.

The rear suspension was a four-bar link setup also using coil springs, a design that was lighter and more compact than the Mustang II's leaf spring Hotchkiss arrangement. Mustangs ordered with the V-8 had a rear anti-roll bar, too. Since the rear bar was used more for lateral location than for controlling sway, the car's roll center was lowered and the rear springs of V-8 Mustangs could be commensurately softer.

The "handling" suspension could be ordered only with 14-inch radials. Compared to the standard set-up, it was tuned for improved handling with higher spring rates, different shock valving, and stiffer bushings. A rear stabilizer bar was also provided when the 2.8-liter V-6 engine was specified.

The "special" suspension included Michelin 190/65R390 TRX tires and forged aluminum wheels which had first appeared on the European Ford Granada. They featured a low-profile wide-aspect configuration for top roadability. According to Ford, the special suspension was designed "to extract maximum performance from this tire/wheel combination." It featured its own shock absorber valving, high rear spring rates, a 1.12-inch front stabilizer bar, and a rear stabilizer bar.

The 1979 Mustang retained the precise rack-and-pinion steering of its predecessor: Power assist was optional. The power system included 1978's variable-ratio rack, which caused steering resistance to decrease as speed dropped. Both manual and power steering gear housings were constructed of die-cast aluminum to keep down weight.

In addition to the 1978 engine offerings—2.3-liter four, 2.8-liter V-6, and 5.0-liter V-8—the 1979 Mustang offered an intriguing new turbocharged version of the standard four. This engine gave a claimed 0-to-55 mph acceleration time of 8.3 seconds with four-speed gearbox, and fuel economy in the mid-20s.

Turbocharging was a new feature for Mustang, but it's been used for a number of years as a way of improving fuel economy and engine efficiency. The principle is simple. A turbine located in the flow of exhaust gases is connected to an impeller (compressor) near the carburetor. During normal driving, the turbine spins too slowly to boost pressure or affect fuel consumption. As the throttle is opened, the engine speeds up which increases the quantity or flow of exhaust gases. The increased flow spins the turbine; the impeller speeds up and increases the density (pressure) of the air-fuel mixture fed to the combustion chambers. The result is an increase in power. To prevent engine damage, maximum boost pressure was limited to 6 pounds per square inch (psi) by an exhaust valve which allowed exhaust gases to bypass the turbine once the 6 psi level was reached.

Minor revisions were made to the 302 V-8 for 1979. It was fitted with a low-restriction exhaust system, used more lightweight components, and featured a ribbed V-belt for the accessory drive. The V-6 engine was in short supply during 1979 and late in the year was replaced by the old 200-cid inline six.

An additional four-speed gearbox was developed for the V-6 and V-8 engines. In effect, it was a three-speed manual transmission with an overdrive fourth gear. Third gear had the direct 1:1 ratio, while fourth had an overdrive ratio of 0.70:1. Final drive ratios were 3.08:1 (automatics, four-speed V-6, and unblown four-cylinder engine), and 3.45:1 (all other drivetrain combinations).

Performance of any particular '79 Mustang naturally depended on the engine and transmission combination fitted. The V-8 was a drag race engine by 1979 standards: 0-to-60 came up in about nine seconds. The V-6's 0-to-60 time was in the 13-14 second range, while the turbocharged four took about 12-12.5 seconds. Press reaction to the various powertrains was mixed. Some writers thought the V-8 was overpowered for the Mustang and out of step in these fuel-short times. The 2.3-liter turbo got the most favorable reviews. As John Dinkel of *Road & Track* put it, "the TRX turbo would seem to be an enthusiast's delight. I just hope that the design compromises dictated by costs and the fact that Ford couldn't start with a completely clean sheet of paper don't wreck that dream. . . There's no doubt the new Mustang has the potential to be the best sporty coupe Ford has ever built, but in some respects (it) is as enigmatic as its predecessor."

There was one more enigma brewing as the press previewed the new Mustang in June, 1978. A month after the previews, Lee A. Iacocca was ousted as president of the Ford Motor Company. Officially, he would take early retirement on October 15th of that year, his 54th birthday.

Many insiders had surmised that Iacocca would be dumped before Henry Ford II himself retired as chief executive in 1980, and as chairman in 1982. But Henry himself had no significant comment. To Iacocca he reportedly said, "It's just one of those things." In removing a strong president, Henry Ford II followed a 50-year company tradition. Past presidents Bull Knudsen, Ernie Breech, and Bunkie Knudsen had all been removed, abruptly, by him or his father.

Iacocca was not bitter, at least not in public. "You just surmise that the Breeches of the world got too big, too soon, and he (Ford) doesn't want strong guys around. You know, he wants to diffuse and bureaucratize the company as he gets to be 61. I guess that's the only thing I can come up with because I really don't have a good sound answer myself."

Ironically, and as Iacocca carefully noted, June, 1978 had been the biggest single month in Ford history. January-to-June had been the biggest six-month period ever and netted the company its largest profit on record. "They probably won't be at this peak again," said Iacocca, "so I guess it's a good time to go."

After 32 years with Ford, Lee Iacocca walked out the door a free agent—but not for long. He was too young and too vigorous to retire. He yearned for a new challenge: He found it. In due course he signed on as president of Chrysler Corporation which he vowed he would pull out of the financial quagmire in which it had been bogged down for so long. A lot of people were pleased by Iacocca's appointment at Chrysler, especially the company's stockholders. As *Automotive News* put it, "Any other auto company would be willing to give up three future draft choices to get its hands on that kind of talent."

Iacocca, said the *AN* editorial, "is a manager, a really professional manager. And he was paid a lot for his services . . . compensation that reached a million dollars a year, figures that defy understanding by mere mortals. Yet, by all standards he earned every penny . . . The job he has done seems to speak for itself." As for the Mustang, Mr. Iacocca's introduction to this book pretty much speaks for itself, too.

Specifications

Model Year Production

No.	Model	1979
02 (66B)	Base 2-door	143,382
03 (61R)	Base 3-door	108,758
04 (66H)	Ghia 2-door	48,788
05 (61H)	Ghia 3-door	31,097
TOTAL		332,025

No.	Model	Price/Weight
02 (66B)	Base 2-door	$4,494/2,530
03 (61R)	Base 3-door	$4,828/2,612
04 (66H)	Ghia 2-door	$5,064/2,648
05 (61H)	Ghia 3-door	$5,216/2,672

General Specifications	1979
Wheelbase:	100.4
Overall length:	179.1
Overall width:	69.1
Std. Trans.:	4-speed manual (4-cyl.) 4-speed manual w/overdrive (V-6 and V-8)
Optional Trans.:	3-speed automatic

Engine Availability Type	CID	HP	1979
I-4	140	88	Std.
Turbo-4	140	NA	Opt.
V-6	171[a]	109	Opt.
V-8	302	140	Opt.

a: replaced mid-1979 by 200-cid I-6

Driving Impressions: Mustang Cobra 2.3 Turbo and 5.0 V-8

Aside from exterior trim and engines, the two 1979 Mustangs we drove couldn't have been more similar. Both were hatchbacks with four-speed gearboxes. Both had the TRX special suspension—optional with the Turbo and standard in the V-8. The key part of the special suspension is the Michelin TRX radial tires mounted on rims designed specifically for them. This suspension option added a hefty $510 to the cost of the car and included extra stiff springs and special shock absorbers as well.

The turbo was decked out in Cobra trim, which consists mainly of matte black finish on the window moldings and lower body. Unfortunately, our car also had the "cobra hood graphics," a big decal of a coiled snake, "California Custom" style. That was a little too much for us, and several times we were tempted to rip the silly thing off. There is really no reason to decorate the car. The big-engine Mustang was in "normal" trim and is quite appealing in appearance without the cartoon. Jack Telnack, who headed the design crew, had prior experience with Ford's German branch in Cologne and the styling of certain German products obviously influenced him. The hatchback Mustang bears a striking resemblance to the Mercedes 450SLC (the notchback even more so), although Telnack has said this wasn't intentional. Maybe not, but it's an interesting stylistic coincidence all the same.

According to Ford there is less than an inch difference in headroom between the two-door notchback coupe and the three-door hatchback. In either case, the Mustang is a cramped car, especially the hatchback which lacks adequate headroom in the back for anyone over about five feet-eight inches tall. At one point we had to carry four passengers for a short distance and found it necessary to run with the hatch open so the people in back could sit upright. A two-plus-two seating package has been part of the Mustang formula since the beginning, however. For those who want better rear seat headroom there's always the Fairmont.

We found the front compartment spacious and comfortable, though the contoured seats still suffer from that long-time Mustang malady of offering no provision for adjusting seatback angle. (This problem was solved in 1980 with the addition of optional reclining bucket seats.) We liked the feeling of the Mustang cockpit even though there are a lot of plastic and vinyl moldings. Ghia models have considerable amounts of fake wood on the dash and doors, but our Mustangs had clean black instrument panels housing easy-to-read gauges with white and green markings. On the Turbo, there is a green warning light to indicate when boost was being supplied (as during hard acceleration) and a red light set to come on when boost exceeds the specified 6 psi maximum. A warning buzzer sounds along with the red warning light, so

Our unadorned '79 Mustang had the V-8 engine.

The "snake" decal on Cobra turbo is gaudy.

Handling with optional TRX tires and special suspension is good on smooth surfaces but bumpy roads upset the ride.

there is no way the driver can miss a turbo malfunction.

There isn't much to say about the Mustang's interior lighting except that it's good. A pull-down reading lamp sheds a broad beam of light over the front compartment without reflecting in the windshield or blinding the driver. There are two courtesy lights as well. The instrument lighting bathed the panel in a pleasant medium green. At night the effect is rather like that of an airplane cockpit because additional lighting is provided for console-mounted controls.

Heating, ventilation, and air conditioning were all first-class. Fresh outside air can be directed to either the footwells or through dashboard vents which can be aimed right at the driver's face. Some federally required devices annoyed us, such as the seat belt reminder light and the raucous buzzer, both of which come on for a few seconds after the car is started if the belts are unfastened. There's another infuriating racket from the ignition key warning buzzer if the driver opens his door without remembering to take the key out first.

The driving position is generally well laid out but there are some aspects that are not executed as well here as in the Mustang's European counterparts. For example, placing the lights and wiper controls on steering column stalks is a good idea: The French and Italians have been doing it for years now. But the Mustang's stalks are more difficult to use than they should be because they're located too far behind the steering wheel. It's amazing the government doesn't pay more attention to things like hard-to-reach controls when drawing up safety legislation instead of all those warning lights and buzzers. And since all of Ford's European models now use stalk controls which are conveniently located and easy to use, it's just as amazing the stalk layout on the Mustang should be so clumsy.

There are a few other clumsy things about the Mustang's interior. The brake pedal is too far off the floor for really smooth heel-and-toe downshifts. The bank of dashboard warning lights, including the all-important turbo lights, are masked by the driver's

hands when the wheel is held at the proper "10-and-2" position. The horn is sounded by pushing inward on the left-hand stalk; why not the more conventional and convenient button on the steering wheel hub? And the hazard flasher was so well hidden we had to consult the owner's manual to find it. When the "key-in" buzzer started screaming in our ears, we tried to pull out the key only to find that a release button mounted on the left-hand side of the steering column had to be unlocked before the key would come out of the ignition. If the government was concerned about a driver's blood pressure rising over aggravations like this, it would have to issue a warning that some of its regulations may be hazardous to our health.

The floor-mounted shift lever for the four-speed manual transmission is conveniently located, and once we solved the puzzle of making all the buzzers stop buzzing we prepared to move off. We tried the Mustang Turbo first. There is no sensation that this car has a turbocharged engine as there is with the Saab Turbo, for example, and there is little turbine whine. The compressor is set to begin providing boost at about 3000 rpm, and our Mustang was so high geared (21 mph per 1000 rpm in top gear) that it took quite a while to reach that speed. Once 3000 is reached some noise can be heard, but performance is as impressive as with the V-6 or V-8. By revving the engine to 4000 rpm to build up some boost before popping the clutch, we just managed to run 0-to-60 in 11.5 seconds. Acceleration in the middle of the speed range is good because engine rpm is high enough for the turbocharger to be really effective.

Our disappointment with the Turbo is its fuel mileage. Over 500 miles of fairly restrained driving we managed only 20 miles per gallon. This wouldn't have been so discouraging if the performance were better, but it isn't. Rivals like the (unblown) VW Scirocco can beat the Mustang in fuel economy in 8-10 mpg, and have better acceleration and passing ability to boot.

The 302-cid V-8 made its final appearance in the Mustang in 1979. It was replaced for 1980 by a smaller and more efficient 255-cid V-8 to help Ford meet corporate average fuel economy (CAFE) standards. Our 302 provided the sort of performance we've come to expect from this classic engine. Most of its driveability problems had been licked over the years. In its '79 application it was smooth throughout the entire rev range, started easily, never hesitated when cold, and was almost inaudible at speed. With the help of the four-speed gearbox, it delivered 0-to-60 acceleration of around nine seconds. Mileage was poor, however, as the V-8 only returned around 15 mpg over 350 miles of driving. This was a disappointment because the 302's four-speed transmission had the high overdrive fourth gear ratio of 0.70:1. It's possible that our car wasn't in the best state of tune. Anyway, the new 255 V-8 should be somewhat more economical.

Both our '79 Mustangs were understeering cars: They tended to keep going forward even when we tried to yank them off the line in a hard corner. But the understeer wasn't excessive and the cars were easily controllable. On a smooth road, their handling was almost faultless—quick, direct, and true, with very little body roll. A bumpy road, however, upsets the suspension's composure. A characteristic of the Michelin TRX tire is its very "square" tread section as it contacts the pavement. This means the wheels must be kept as close to vertical on the road surface as possible for the tires to provide their best grip. An uneven or rutted surface upset our TRX suspensions, and wheel jounce on bad bumps was particularly noticeable.

The "third revolution" Mustang is beautifully styled. And with a few exceptions, its ergonomics and interior design are the equal of many European cars. The latest Mustang also offers more comfort and less surface glitter compared to the Mustang II. Handling is good, though it could have been better. The Turbo's performance was a disappointment: A V-6 Mustang with four-speed can easily outrun the Turbo, and would probably turn in equally good gas mileage. Unfortunately, the short supply of V-6s in 1979 restricted their availability to cars equipped with automatic transmission only. In late 1979, with continuing supply problems, Ford dropped the V-6 from the Mustang engine lineup.

Specifications

	1979 Mustang Cobra Turbo	1979 Mustang Cobra 302
Price when new:	$6,350	$6,201
Engine type, cylinders:	ohc I-4	ohv V-8
Bore x Stroke (in.):	3.78x3.13	4.00x3.00
Displacement (cu. in.):	140	302
Compression ratio:	9.0:1	9.0:1
Horsepower @ rpm:	130 (net) @ 5400	133 (net) @ 3600
Transmission type/forward gears:	manual/4	manual/4
Final drive ratio:	3.45:1	3.08:1
Tire size:	190/65HR390	190/65HR390
Steering, turns lock-to-lock:	3.0 (power)	3.0 (power)
Turning diameter (ft.):	39.0	39.0
Brake swept area (sq. in.):	248.0	248.0
Curb weight (lbs.):	2776	2850
Weight distribution, front/rear:	58/42	61/29
Wheelbase (in.):	100.4	100.4
Overall length (in.):	179.1	179.1
Overall width (in.):	69.1	69.1
Track, front/rear (in.):	55.6/57.0	55.6/57.0
Height (in.):	51.8	51.8
Ground clearance (in.):	5.0	5.0
Suspension, front:	McPherson struts, lower A-arms; coil springs; anti-roll bar; tube shocks	
Suspension, rear:	Trailing arms, upper angled arms; coil springs; anti-roll bar; tube shocks	
Performance pounds/horsepower (net):	21.7	20.5
acceleration, 0-60 mph (sec.)	11.5	9.0
estimated top speed (mph)	105.0	115.0

Anniversary Year: 1980

"Improving the Breed" is the theme at Ford for 1980 as Mustang celebrates its 15th anniversary. And improved it is—unquestionably for the better. The six-cylinder engine is now available with four-speed gearbox offering an excellent compromise between the performance of the V-8 and the economy of the four along with the fun of a manual transmission. A new 255 cubic-inch V-8 is offered—lighter and more efficient than the 302 it replaces. Styling has changed in detail only. Nobody at Ford was unhappy about the looks of the '79 cars, and neither were the customers. Altogether, the Anniversary Mustang is more refined than the '79 model and may be the best Mustang yet.

Ford's ponycar paced the Indianapolis 500 in 1979, so it was natural an "Indy Pace car" replica would appear as a mid-year addition to the line. The pace car look has been applied to the Cobra package for 1980 which now includes front and rear spoilers, integral fog lamps, a restyled grille, and a non-functional hood scoop. Standard on the Cobra is the TRX special

suspension and the turbocharged 2.3-liter four-cylinder engine. Also available with the new 255-cid V-8, the Cobra package is offered on the hatchback body style only.

The standard two-door notchback now comes standard with high-back all-vinyl bucket seats and color-keyed interior and door trim. As before, all Mustangs have complete instrumentation and P-metric radial tires. The equipment in 1979's Sport Option, which was listed as a separate model, is now included as standard on the three-door hatchback. It consists of styled sport wheels with bright trim rings, black rocker panel and window moldings, wide bodyside moldings, striped rub strip extensions, and a sporty steering wheel. On all models halogen-type headlights have replaced conventional tungsten sealed beams.

Ghia models continue their tradition of luxury. Color-keyed components are plentiful: seat belts, mirrors, bodyside moldings, and the C-pillars on hatchbacks. All Ghias feature low-back vinyl bucket

1980 Mustang Turbo with Cobra option

CONSUMER GUIDE®

1980 Mustang hardtop with "carriage roof" option

seats with headrests, door map pockets, a visor vanity mirror, thicker pile carpeting, a deluxe steering wheel, roof-mounted assist handles, and a full complement of interior lights. Available on Ghias is a choice of leather or cloth-and-vinyl upholstery in six different colors.

The 1980 option list is as extensive as ever. Among the extra-cost items are a tilt steering wheel, speed control, power door locks, inside remote trunk release, rear window wiper-washer, flip-up sunroof, and a wide assortment of wheels, wheel covers, and audio equipment. Available for all models are the Recaro reclining front bucket seats first introduced on the 1979 Indy

With the new "carriage roof," Mustang has the look of a convertible with top up.

1980 Mustang **Turbo** with Cobra option.

Pace Car replica. These seats have an infinitely variable seatback reclining adjustment and more thigh support padding. No longer can Mustang be accused of lagging behind its European competition.

Other 1980 options are a roof-mounted luggage carrier, a window shade-type cargo area cover for the hatchback, and accent side tape stripes. An interesting styling option for notchbacks is the carriage roof which includes a diamond-grain full vinyl roof cover plus black door and quarter window frames and moldings. Designed to simulate the top-up appearance of a true convertible, the carriage roof shows how handsome a soft-top version of the new Mustang would be, if only Ford could be persuaded to revive this body style.

The 1980 model offers one of the broadest selection of engines and transmissions in Mustang history. The lineup consists of a 2.3-liter (140-cid) ohv four with or without turbocharger; a 3.3-liter (200-cid) six, and a 4.2-liter (255-cid) V-8. The fours come with a conventional four-speed manual transmission, while the six uses the manual four-speed overdrive gearbox. Automatic transmission is standard on the V-8 and optional with all other engines.

Ford brought back the efficient 200-cid six during the latter part of the 1979 model year because supplies of V-6s from Europe weren't adequate. The inline six features a seven main-bearing crankshaft, hydraulic valve lifters, a cast-iron block, and a one-barrel carburetor. A simple, easy-to-service engine, it yields performance similar to the V-6 it replaced. According to Ford's "Cost-of-Ownership" formula, where required maintenance for the first 50,000 miles is averaged according to dealer parts and labor prices, the inline six costs the buyer less to operate than the V-6.

1979½ Mustang Indy Pace Car replica

The 255-cid V-8 is the latest in a long line of Ford small-block engines, which began with the 221-cid Fairlane V-8 of 1962. The rationale for this powerplant is obvious: Ford needs to meet government CAFE (corporate average fuel economy) standards and the 255 engine gives better fuel economy than the larger 302 V-8 used in '79, but at the expense of some loss in performance.

The Mustang has been with us now for 15 years. Are the latest versions really that different from the original 1965 Mustangs? From a study of certain vital statistics, it would be tempting to say little has changed:

Major Statistics	1965 Mustang	1979 Mustang
length (in)	181.6	179.1
width (in)	68.2	69.1
wheelbase (in)	108.0	100.4
weight, 6 cyl coupe (lb)	2,445	2,516
base six, cid	200	200
base V-8, cid	260	255

But in another sense, today's Mustang is far more advanced than the 1965 model. Even though the figures above are very similar, they tell only part of the story. The '79 has about the same overall length as the '65 and its wheelbase is 7.6 inches shorter—yet it has the same amount of passenger room up front, and offers more rear seat room. Obviously Ford has learned much about space utilization since 1965. Although the '79 has all the current mandatory safety features, like reinforced doors and "five-mph" bumpers, it weighs hardly more than a comparable 1965 Mustang. Ford has also learned much about the use of lightweight materials and construction techniques over the past 15 years.

There are some interesting comparisons in the engine department, too. The 2.3-liter four, of course, is not comparable to any Mustang engine of 1965. The six, however, is exactly the same powerplant offered in '65 (except for the early cars, which had a 170-cid unit). The 255 V-8 is derived from the 302 which, in turn, was developed from the 289 and which itself was enlarged from the original Mustang's 260 V-8. The Ford small-blocks have a long pedigree. Yet both the six and the V-8 get better fuel mileage than their 1965 counterparts and have comparable performance. The only drawback to these engines is that, since 1965, they have been reworked to use unleaded gas, which is wasteful of resources in a way unrelated to car or driver. (It takes 15 percent more crude oil to make a gallon of unleaded regular than to make a gallon of leaded regular.) The continuing shortage of crude oil may eventually lead to a reconsideration of emission laws which most car makers now meet by catalytic converters and unleaded gas.

What the comparison charts don't show is the long, long road Mustang has travelled between 1965 and 1980. Along the way, Mustang became one of the world's fastest four-place production cars; it also became much too large, too unwieldy, and too wasteful of resources. That the lighter and more efficient 1980

1980 Mustang hardtop

Mustang so closely resembles the '65 in size and performance is perhaps a coincidence. Then again, perhaps it isn't. We had a lot of automotive decisions to make in the late 1960's and, looking back, it seems we generally made the wrong ones. Most everyone agrees that the Mustang changed for the worse after 1968.

But hindsight is cheap and far too easily indulged. Enthusiasts may take heart from the 1980 Mustang. It proves that Americans *can* build nimble, handsome, efficient automobiles that are fun to drive over a bit of winding road. After 15 years the original ponycar has come full circle. Mustang is again the kind of car it was in the beginning.

Specifications

1980 Models			Prices/Weights	
02	(66B)	Base 2-door	$ NA	2606
03	(61R)	Base 3-door	$ NA	2614
04	(66H)	Ghia 2-door	$ NA	NA
05	(61H)	Ghia 3-door	$ NA	NA

General Specifications	1980
Wheelbase:	100.4
Overall length:	179.1
Overall width:	69.1
Std. Trans.:	4-speed manual (4-cyl.) 4-speed overdrive manual (6-cyl.) 3-speed automatic (8-cyl.)
Optional Trans.:	3-speed automatic

Engine Availability			1979
Type	CID	HP	
I-4	140	88	Std.
Turbo-4	140	NA	Opt.
I-6	200	NA	Opt.
V-8	255	NA	Opt.

Clubs for the Mustang Enthusiast

Mustang Owners Club

The Mustang Owners Club is an international organization formed in 1975 and has grown to over 500 members. Membership is broad based in the United States, and represented as well in Australia, New Zealand, Canada, Great Britain, Sweden, Norway, Iceland, and Switzerland.

The main objective of the Mustang Owners Club is to promote and preserve 1965-73 Mustangs. Nevertheless, some members own Mustang IIs, 1979-80 models, Mercury Cougars, or other Ford cars. A member does not actually have to own a Mustang—

enthusiasm is the only requirement.

The club publishes a monthly newsletter, *The Pony Express,* which covers Mustang history, technology, the future of the marque, restoration, and maintenance. A "spotlight series" covers individual models or years and lists factory standard and optional equipment. The series discusses the market situation at the time the model was produced, and all other pertinent information. Members' cars are featured in a series entitled "Mustang of the Month." Meeting and car show information is provided and reports on past events are numerous. *The Pony Express* also contains a large

A herd of potent ponies is coralled at this Shelby American Auto Club convention.

classified section, where members may run ads for cars and parts, literature, and other Mustang paraphernalia.

The Ford Motor Company often calls on the club to provide Mustang information to owners who write to Dearborn. The club maintains an extensive library, including shop manuals, sales and marketing literature, and monthly auto magazines. The club has also provided information and assistance to authors.

Several local chapters have been established, and more are being planned. Local chapters encourage group activities such as picnics, tours, shows, and other events. Family participation is emphasized. Monthly meetings are held in each area. There are also large regional meets. Club members are Mustang enthusiasts of all ages who own everything from placid sixes, to fire-breathing Shelbys and Boss 302s, to luxury Grandes. With all the options available, it is probable that no two Mustangs were ever exactly alike—there is a car for just about everybody.

Membership dues in the Mustang Owners Club are $10 per year. For further information on the club, contact the president, Paul G. McLaughlin, 2829 Cagua Drive NE, Albuquerque, New Mexico 87110.

Shelby American Auto Club

Though the great automobiles of Carroll Shelby were built for only a few years, they made a statement powerful enough to affect virtually every subsequent performance car. Shelbys were not the kind of cars enthusiasts forget. Shelby American and its products touched every corner of the motorsport world. In addition to building the Shelby-Mustang, the company was victorious in almost every type of competition event: Road racing, drags, autocrosses, and rallies. Shelby American was responsible for the Sunbeam Tiger, the Ford GT program and its 1966-67 LeMans victories, the Mustang Trans-Am and Can-Am racers, and much of the Boss 302. Carroll Shelby also left his mark on performance equipment from manifolds and valve covers to wheels and tachometers.

The Shelby American Auto Club was founded in late 1975. It was dedicated to the preservation, care, history, and enjoyment of Shelby products. With a national leadership well versed in public relations and advertising, the club's membership grew to over 5,000 within three years.

The membership is made up of enthusiasts and owners of all types of Ford-powered performance cars. The value of the cars themselves has risen thanks to the enthusiasm generated by SAAC. All the cars from Shelby American, as well as other Ford performance cars, are among the most desirable in the world. Almost every one is a blue chip investment that will never be worth less than it is today. Happily, Shelby parts are once again available, if you know where to look. The club knows, and makes this information available to members.

Every major population center in the country has an active SAAC region. Meets, car shows, autocrosses, open track events, and picnics are all scheduled and

1965 Shelby GT-350

run by members. Each summer the club's four-day national convention attracts thousands of members and hundreds of cars. Conventions feature technical seminars, guest speakers, parts swaps, films, historical displays, and cocktail parties.

The club's bimonthly magazine, *The Shelby American,* is one of the most respected periodicals in its field. Each issue contains more than 60 pages of technical information, photos, historical and general-interest articles, lists of parts sources, and question-and-answer columns. There are four to six pages of classified ads, which are free to members. A national calendar of events keeps members informed of happenings in all areas.

New members receive a membership packet containing dash plaque, club decal, membership card, and certificate. SAAC operates a nationwide hotline for reporting stolen cars and is tied in to 5,000 detectives throughout the country. The club publishes special books dealing with technical aspects of Shelby American cars as well as owner registries.

Ownership of a Shelby product is not required for membership—just enthusiasm. A free brochure is available. Membership rates are $19.95 (magazine by third class mail) or $26.95 (magazine by first class mail). Write Rick Kopec, director, 24-C April Lane, Norwalk, Connecticut 06850 for information.

Acknowledgements

The preparation of this book has been made possible, and easier, through the kind assistance of numerous individuals and organizations.

Our sincere thanks for his introductory statement to Lee A. Iacocca, now chairman of Chrysler Corporation, but still known as the father of the Mustang, the Mustang II, and the "third revolution" Mustangs of 1979-80. He brings to Chrysler the same enthusiasm, realism, and imaginative product planning he demonstrated at Ford, and we wish him well in his new position.

We are grateful also to the assistance of the men and women of Ford Motor Company. Those who provided quotes, answered our questions, and offered other assistance are too numerous to mention here, but have been noted throughout this book. William Carroll of Ford Public Relations made it possible for us to research the company's comprehensive design archives; G. Donald Adams, Manager Print Media Services at the Henry Ford Museum and Greenfield Village, spent a considerable amount of time viewing and selecting those photographs for us. Other photographs in this book were provided by the Ford Photomedia Department. The driving impressions photographs of the '57 Thunderbird, '65 Mustang, '66 and '67 Shelbys were provided by the authors. Our thanks also to Bruce Haun and the Sports Car Club of America for their assistance in photographic research for the competition chapter.

The biographical sketch of Lee Iacocca in Chapter 2, and the Mustang development story in Chapter 3, were written by Michael Lamm and originally published in *Special-Interest Autos,* September-October, 1974. Driving impressions of the Shelby-Mustangs and the history of the Shelby-Mustang were written by Rick Kopec. Chapter 13 ("Competition Mustangs") was excerpted in part from Rick Kopec's book, "*Shelby American Guide,*" published in 1978. All other text was written by Richard M. Langworth. The '57 Thunderbird-'65 Mustang driving impressions originally appeared in *Cars & Parts,* February 1977. Previously published material is used with the permission of the copyright owners.

We could not have provided the four driving impressions in this book without the help and cooperation of the cars' owners. The 1957 Thunderbird and 1965 Mustang GT were provided by James Northup of Princeton, New Jersey. The 1966 Shelby GT-350 is owned by author Rick Kopec of Norwalk, Connecticut. The 1967 Shelby GT-350 was provided by David Mathews of Guilford, Connecticut. The Mustang II and 1979 Mustangs were provided by the Ford Motor Company. Our thanks to the enthusiasts who have maintained these cars in like-new condition.

Mustang I